the
style diary
of a
Bollywood diva

Born into the first family of Bollywood, Kareena Kapoor has already spent a
lifetime in the spotlight. While her screen presence in movies like *Jab We Met*,
3 Idiots, *Chameli* and *Kabhi Khushi Kabhie Gham* has earned consistent praise
from critics, her glamorous style is loved and instantly copied by millions
of fans. This is her first official book.

Journalist and fashion writer Rochelle Pinto was given her first column,
Bewear, in a national daily at the age of twenty. It became popular for its
irreverent decimation of celebrity wardrobes, earning her enough notoriety
to get noticed by publisher Shobhaa Dé. This is her debut book.

Shobhaa Dé Books is a special imprint created by one
of Penguin India's best-loved and highest-selling authors.
The list will feature celebrity authors handpicked by Shobhaa,
and will focus on lifestyle, business, cinema and people.

the
style diary
of a
bollywood diva

KAREENA
KAPOOR

with Rochelle Pinto

Sdé

Shobhaa Dé
BOOKS

SHOBHAA DÉ BOOKS
Penguin Books India Pvt. Ltd, 11 Community Centre, Panchsheel Park,
New Delhi 110 017, India
Penguin Group (USA) Inc., 375 Hudson Street, New York, New York 10014, USA
Penguin Group (Canada), 90 Eglinton Avenue East, Suite 700, Toronto,
Ontario, M4P 2Y3, Canada (a division of Pearson Penguin Canada Inc.)
Penguin Books Ltd, 80 Strand, London WC2R 0RL, England
Penguin Ireland, 25 St Stephen's Green, Dublin 2, Ireland
(a division of Penguin Books Ltd)
Penguin Group (Australia), 707 Collins Street, Melbourne, Victoria 3008, Australia
(a division of Pearson Australia Group Pty Ltd)
Penguin Group (NZ), 67 Apollo Drive, Rosedale, North Shore 0632,
New Zealand (a division of Pearson New Zealand Ltd)
Penguin Group (South Africa) (Pty) Ltd, 24 Sturdee Avenue, Rosebank,
Johannesburg 2196, South Africa

Penguin Books Ltd, Registered Offices: 80 Strand, London WC2R 0RL, England

First published in Shobhaa Dé Books by Penguin Books India 2012

Copyright © Kareena Kapoor 2012
Illustrations copyright © Joy Gosney 2012
Front cover image: photograph by Prasad Naik; hair and make-up by Subhash Vagal;
costume by Tanya Ghaveri. Back cover image: photograph courtesy Lavie Handbags;
make-up by Mallika Bhatt; hair by Pompy Hans

Pages 271 and 272 are an extension of the copyright page

ISBN 9780143417279

Designed by Marina Bang
Printed at Thomson Press India Ltd, New Delhi

ALWAYS LEARNING   **PEARSON**

Now it's your time
to shine girls!

♡n
style,
Kareena
Kapoor

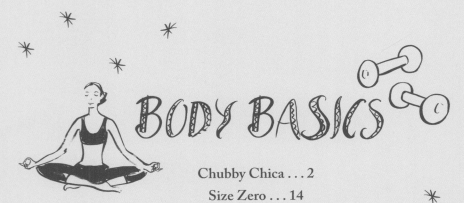

BODY BASICS

FASHION FABULOUS

BEAUTY TRUTHS

MAN POWER

BODY BASICS

CHUBBY CHICA

I used to be just Bebo, the girl next door. Both Lolo and I lived a pretty regular middle-class life in South Mumbai. Our weekends were spent between going to church with Mom and swimming with our friends at the Breach Candy club. That was as far as our diva upbringing went! The only time I would be the centre of attention was on 21 September: my birthday. But even then it was the Goriawala Care Bear birthday cake which was the real star of the party, not me. It was the one indulgence my parents would allow me, without any fuss.

Even when we moved to Lokhandwala when Lolo became an actress, they would get the cake delivered all the way home. Everybody who knew me at that time will tell you this was the high point of my life!

People seem to think that I had some sort of pampered-princess upbringing, with a hundred attendants waiting on me hand and foot. I wish! My closest brush with the world of glamour as a child was watching my grandmother get dressed to go to the Cricket Club of India. Every time she began to get ready, I would sit right beside her and

I may have looked like a girlie girl with pink cheeks and long hair, but in my heart of hearts I was a complete tomboy.

watch her every move. I will never forget how daintily she applied her bright red Lakme lipstick. As soon as she was out the front door, I'd rush to her room try on the lipstick myself, and strike silly poses in front of the mirror. Then I'd beg my mom to bring out the camcorder and film me dancing to a Sridevi song.

As I grew older, the naughty streak in me kicked into high gear. I never got into trouble with the teachers, but I became notorious in school for being a complete firebrand. I may have looked like a girlie girl with pink cheeks and

long hair, but in my heart of hearts I was a complete tomboy. I wouldn't even hesitate to get into a fight, especially if they had insulted someone I was close to. Some things never change; I'm still as protective about the people I love. But I think I've quite outgrown the physical violence bit!

We were a close group of friends, always hanging out at each other's houses or in the building compound. Once in a while, we'd sneak off to Dig Inn in Bandra or Candies at Pali Hill to snack on their still popular chicken sandwiches. My mom's list of dos and

I would get together with my friend Reena and sneak my 118 NE out and go for little drives.

don'ts included my not straying too far away from home. By the time I was a teenager, she was travelling a lot with Lolo. So the rule was enforced with even more gusto but it also meant she couldn't keep an eye on me 24/7! At that age, there was no way I was going to pass up this window of opportunity.

Whenever my mom was out on a shoot with Lolo, I would get together with my friend Reena and sneak my 118 NE out and go for little drives. Of course, for all our mischief, we also had the wonderful knack of getting caught, almost every time. One day, we happily snuck the car out when Mom was out on a long trip. We were so pleased with ourselves! Finally, we were going to get away with our little scam. Obviously, we had no idea what

we were in for. Reena was teaching me to drive on Pali Hill, when suddenly, we saw HDIL builder Sunny Dewan coming down the road in our direction. I froze, lost control and boom! We had crashed headlong into his expensive car. I don't know what I was more scared of: banging into someone else's car, or the thought that if my mother found out, she would ground me for life. But Sunny, being the gentleman that he is, offered to pay for the damages himself so that I wouldn't get into trouble. Phew!

But then, as if things couldn't get any worse, just as we returned home after sneaking the car back into the garage, we got the biggest shock of our teenage lives! There was my mom, sitting at the dinner table, patiently

waiting to catch her rascal daughter red-handed. I was grounded: no going out, no hanging out with my friends, no phone calls, just head buried in my school books for a whole month.

When I wasn't trying to sneak the car out, I was trying to sneak some street food in. Like most kids, we were only allowed to eat home-cooked food because my mother was very particular about our health. Even french fries, which anybody will tell you is my single most-favourite meal in the whole world, was made from scratch in my mom's kitchen. My regular routine after school was sitting with my plate of fries and ketchup in front of the TV, watching *Dynasty* or a good Hindi movie. Our school tiffins were jam or marmalade sandwiches with an apple. No canteen

food for the Kapoor girls! But of course, whenever I got the chance, I'd sneak out to the crushed-ice-gola stall or the roadside paani puri wala on Pali Hill. The sev puris were my favourite, and he knew how to make them exactly like I wanted them: extra spicy. I never told my mother, but I guess I didn't have to. She always found out because I would always fall sick the very next day, and get a 'serves you right' from her. When I look back at that time, I'm so grateful to my parents for making sure that I grew up as a normal kid. I got to enjoy the best of both worlds, and I wouldn't change a minute of it.

While I was the firebrand brat, Lolo was the exact opposite of me. As the elder one, she has always been more reserved and proper. I'm sure

My parents thank their stars that at least one daughter didn't give them grey hair before their time.

my parents thank their stars that at least one daughter didn't give them grey hair before their time. Lolo was always very careful about revealing her thoughts and feelings. She would only do so when she was absolutely comfortable with her surroundings. I, on the other hand, was and, I think, am still quite famous for saying whatever pops into my head. Without thinking twice about what I'm saying or whom I'm saying it to.

Though, I have to say Lolo is undoubtedly the coolest elder sister anyone could have. She never ignored me or treated me like the annoying kid-sister who wanted to follow her everywhere. In fact, she indulged me quite a bit, taking me around and letting me hang out with her friends. Since she was already earning her own money, I was the beneficiary. She was probably the person who introduced me to the beautiful world of fashion that I would soon fall completely in love with. She bought me my first piece of designer clothing ever! It was this gorgeous Jean Paul Gaultier newspaper print see-through top. My friends were even more excited than I once they saw the label. Any special occasion and I would wear my Gaultier top and feel like an absolute star!

Because of our six-year age gap, I was still a child when Lolo joined the movies. But I'd accompany her to the sets as often as I could. Which basically meant as often as my mom would allow me! I couldn't wait to get a chance to visit the set and watch all the drama and fun that went on behind the scenes. Lolo was the sexy

new actress being romanced by all the hottest male stars of that time, always the centre of attention. We'd go absolutely crazy spotting all our favourite heroes. I had a huge crush on Akshaye Khanna at the time, and would literally blush from head to toe whenever he was around.

I was so starry-eyed at that time, but the famous Kareena confidence gene didn't stop me from telling anyone who'd listen that I was also going to be as famous an actress one day. Salman still teases me about this, because he was the one who indulged my kiddie fantasies the most by actually chatting with me. Salman was also probably the coolest one of Lolo's co-stars. Once he

was in an especially generous mood and decided to take all of us to his house to sample his mom's famous mutton biryani. I mean, literally, all the guys on set and an entourage of my friends, who could not believe their luck. The whole gang climbed into his giant open Gypsy, and drove straight from the sets of *Andaaz Apna Apna* at Mehboob studio in Bandra to his house in Galaxy Apartments. I think Salma Aunty was quite shocked to see so many hungry mouths at her doorstep. But she's such a great host and, of course, the most fantastic cook. I'll never forget that day because my friends and I got to dine with the superstar himself! And today, we have

one of the biggest hits in Bollywood, *Bodyguard*, to our credit. If you went back in time and told thirteen-year-old Kareena this was going to happen, she'd probably faint with excitement.

Looking back at that time, I realize that though my life has changed on the outside, on the inside, it's absolutely the same. Just because I'm an actress now doesn't mean I act like a starry diva who has a bunch of rules for others to follow and throws a tantrum every few minutes. I may have had the sexiest bodyguard

ever on screen, but in real life, I refuse to hire personal security in Mumbai. This is the city I was born and grew up in, and I've never felt unsafe here. I know that my bank account allows me to drape myself in couture from head to toe, even when I'm sleeping. But I'm still most comfortable in my Citizens of Humanity jeans and Topshop ganjis, even if they're not the most expensive things to wear. I see my face on magazine covers and movie posters, Photoshopped to perfection. But on my own time, I

To me, style is not about designer labels or expensive jewellery . . . It's more about loving the way you look, and having the confidence to be who you are.

have my hair up in a ponytail and not a drop of make-up on my face.

To me, style is not about designer labels or expensive jewellery, though they do often help polish the whole package. It's more about loving the way you look, and having the confidence to be who you are without trying to copy someone else. I know it's a cliché that you've probably heard a thousand times. But it's really the mantra I swear by. The secret to gaining confidence is simple: treat yourself the way you deserve to be

treated. That could mean exercising and eating right because your body needs to be fit and healthy, or splurging on a new Valentino gown and those delicious red heels because you've worked hard and deserve a treat. It could even be spending quality time with that one person who makes you feel like you're the centre of his universe.

Take it from someone who's spent more than a decade in the movie business: you don't need to be an actress to feel like a star!

SIZE ZERO

You know how some people are just dying to turn eighteen so they can finally drive, vote and/or move into their own apartment? Well, I couldn't wait to grow up so that I could make my acting debut. When I signed on *Kaho Naa . . . Pyaar Hai* opposite Rakesh Roshan's handsome, young, and at that time completely unknown, son Hrithik, I still had every ounce of my puppy fat intact. But at that time, it really wasn't a big deal, and nobody told me I was looking too fat or needed to lose weight. I was so confident that I was convinced I had a great figure. As fate would have it, I didn't go on to do that movie and J.P. Dutta's *Refugee* turned out to be my launch vehicle in 2000 with Jaya and Amitabh Bachchan's then unknown son Abhishek! I learned overnight that the camera really does add a few kilos. So now, instead of dancing around my bedroom without a care, I was dancing on an unforgiving 70 mm screen. But who cared. It was too much fun to be living the fabulous big Bollywood dream.

I even scored the *Filmfare* award for Best Female Debut, which was the icing on the cake. My dream was coming true, and I couldn't have loved my life more!

Throughout this time, fitness wasn't high up on my list of priorities. Let's face it; I was never the sporty type.

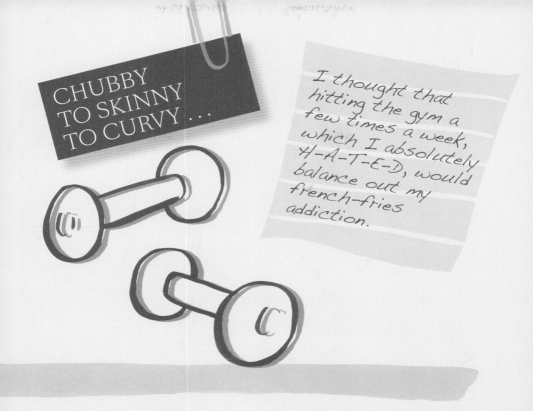

CHUBBY TO SKINNY TO CURVY ...

I thought that hitting the gym a few times a week, which I absolutely H-A-T-E-D, would balance out my french-fries addiction.

In *Refugee*, I was the cute, slightly chubby girl next door. My puppy fat worked for the character and brought her alive. To be honest, I wouldn't have had it any other way. I'm glad I wasn't obsessed with being stick-thin as a teenager, because that gave me a chance to enjoy every silly thing that I can't even dream of doing now.

But the teenage dream was over and chubby cheeks wouldn't work for all my characters. Back then, I thought that hitting the gym a few times a week, which I absolutely H-A-T-E-D, would balance out my french-fries addiction. In my mind this was an excruciating fitness regime. And it even worked for some time: I actually dropped a few kilos and had a super-flat belly to prove it. This was around the time I signed on *Asoka* with none other than the King Khan himself! For *Asoka* I was curvy but in form because my character was dressed throughout in barely-there white saris and cholis. In fact, after baring my midriff in that red bustier and pants for *You are my Soniya* in Karan Johar's *Kabhi Khushi Kabhie Gham*, I received endless compliments about my figure. In my head I was doing absolutely brilliantly when it came to my body.

But then my movies hit a rough patch. With *Main Prem Ki Diwaani Hoon*, *Mujhse Dosti Karoge* and *LOC Kargil* all sinking at the box office, my

Yoga may look peaceful and calming, but even Arnold Schwarzenegger would have trouble breathing after twenty surya namaskars in a row.

focus was diverted from working on my body to improving my body of work. Trying to figure out my own path to success took up all my time. Which is probably why keeping track of the numbers on the weighing scale was the last thing on my mind.

But I have to admit through it all, my fans have always been super supportive. Even when I hit 64 kilos in 2006, not ideal for a 5'5" frame, nobody ever told me I was too fat to be a leading lady. Besides, I wasn't going to be baring it all in a bikini, right? WRONG!

In 2007, my life changed forever. I signed on *Tashan*, a fullon glamorous masala movie, with two of the hottest and fittest actors around: Akshay Kumar and Saif Ali Khan. And me, rising out of the sea like a Bond girl, wearing nothing but a green bikini.

This was completely new territory for me. So, when I looked into the mirror to decide whether I really had the body to pull this off, I had to be honest with myself. I realized I was going to be showing off a lot more than just my acting skills. What did I do? I panicked.

I had nightmares of how my love handles would be on display for the whole world to see. I was determined to do something that would shock the entire industry. Something every woman secretly wants to do: become super thin and fit, and have that perfect bikini bod!

Until then, I had tried a few yoga classes with Payal Gidwani from Bharat Thakur's academy, but just like I warned her on the first day, I soon got bored and quit. I would hit the gym off and on but I barely had a fitness regime in

chocolates and french fries. Even my secret loot hidden on the top shelf.

My junk food de-addiction had begun. I will admit, though, the first few days were pure torture. I spent my time daydreaming about mountains of masala-topped potato chips. The hardest thing to do was change my perception of food. I had grown up in a proper Punjabi household, where ghee equals love. I was taught the fattier and meatier the food, the better it is. I was taught to look at my meals as building blocks for my new figure. There was no way a flat stomach was going to develop if I continued to gorge on oily, greasy snacks. It wasn't easy but I was determined to eat right and stay on track. So I sucked it up and became my dietician's disciple.

Since gymming clearly wasn't my thing, I went right back to Payal, and told her I needed some yoga magic. This time around I was committed and I had made up my mind to stick it out, no matter what.

But oh my God, the first class was pure torture. Yoga may look peaceful and calming, but even Arnold Schwarzenegger would have trouble breathing after twenty surya namaskars in a row. Payal had to physically lift my legs into the asanas and help me balance because I felt so heavy. It would have been embarrassing if it hadn't looked so funny. But two weeks into my booty boot camp, and my

place. As for my diet, turning vegetarian was the one thing that had helped me drop some of the extra kilos. But I was still very far away from being in shape. I desperately needed something which would give my weight-loss programme a turbo boost.

That's when my friend Shaira Khan told me about a genie called Rujuta Diwekar. She was a brilliant trainer at Sykes Gym, where Shaira worked out, and I was told that she helped her clients by prescribing diets to them along with their exercises. This was around the time I was shooting for *Yeh mera dil* in *Don 2*, and was probably at my plumpest. Rujuta stormed into my life like a whirlwind. We met and chatted for a bit, and I signed up for her weight-loss programme. The next thing I knew, she was in my house, discarding my stash of banana chips,

Magazine editors were the most excited because finally there was an Indian actress who could wear the sexiest of clothes and they didn't have to Photoshop all the flab.

stamina and flexibility slowly started improving. More than that, I began to enjoy it. Soon, I was able to do ten surya namaskars in a row without even breaking into a sweat, and I would happily take on whatever punishing asanas Payal prescribed.

The combination of my controlled vegetarian diet and intense yoga sessions started working its way into my body. I saw myself shrink every ten days. My arms, legs and abs looked ribbed. I felt fit, empowered and super hot.

I had dropped ten kilos in ten months, and my waistline went from 28 to 24 inches. Muscles appeared from under layers of puppy fat, and my collar bones made their debut appearance. I was even shopping in the kids' section in departmental stores because they didn't have my size in the adults' section!

I shot the now-famous bikini scene and I must admit I was a bundle of nerves! But soon the shot was ready, the film was complete and the promos hit the screen. The very next day my photos were all over every newspaper, magazine, TV channel and website. And everybody seemed to love the new me! It felt like the whole nation was tuned in to my weighing scale, and they were tracking my calorie count like it was the Sensex. That's when it hit me. I had officially become Kareena 'Size Zero' Kapoor. And so, the size-zero syndrome had officially begun.

Everything I wore, even the most daring clothes straight off the ramp, looked super hot. Magazine editors were the most excited because finally there was an Indian actress who could wear the sexiest of clothes and they didn't have to Photoshop all the flab.

My photos were all over every newspaper, magazine and TV channel.

Every red-carpet appearance was being dissected and discussed in the media, not to mention fan blogs and Facebook. Honestly, I had no idea what Size Zero meant. I learnt about it from reading the newspaper, where they said that only the top models in Paris had those measurements. Six-foot-tall supermodels … and me! People had started thinking of me as a model, though I am nowhere near being one. All the clothes I wore both on screen and off were flying off the shelves because women wanted the exact-same look.

My mother, who was always supportive, would tease me saying that I was disappearing right before her eyes. She used to ask Payal, whom she jokingly called Hitler, 'What are you doing to my Bebo? There's no difference between her front and back anymore!'

That was also the time I met Saif Ali Khan. I was at the peak of the lean phase. He was everything a girl could dream of: handsome, chivalrous and a complete gentleman with a wicked sense of humour. One night, after pack-up, he asked me out to dinner. There we were, enjoying our main course, and he turned to me and said, 'I've never seen an Indian woman with a razor-sharp jawline like yours.' It's still one of the best compliments he's ever given me. Let me repeat that. We were at dinner. I was still eating, in fact, more than ever before!

Rujuta was adamant that the only way to lose weight was through food. She is strict but sensible and practical. She customized my diet plan to suit my palate, lifestyle and needs. Being vegetarian helped, because I felt lighter and more active (though I must admit

I had made my decision: I was going to put on weight. I made my second big decision regarding my weight: I would become my ideal, perfect size. So goodbye, Size Zero. It was time to get my curves back.

Find a diet plan to suit your palate, lifestyle and needs.

I missed my french fries!). She put me on a diet plan which had me eating every two hours. Of course, there were funny stories floating everywhere and people were talking about how I was only allowed to have one orange a day. And I don't even like oranges!

I think some people forget that I'm a working professional, with a pretty tough schedule. If I was starving and shooting around the clock at the same time, I would have landed in hospital by the second week. And as I mentioned earlier, it took me ten months to get into shape. That's close to a year, and I don't think any human being can survive on an orange a day for that long! Especially not me, I'm a khati-piti Punjabi kudi: I need my food and a lot of it. I was on a diet definitely but one that had me eating and keeping healthy.

Looking back at that crazy phase, I have a feeling no matter how many hit films I deliver, these two words 'Size Zero' will remain my legacy. Somewhere, I just wanted to prove that a hardcore Punjabi who smothers everything in ghee could also look like a model if she really set her mind to it. Of course, maintaining a 24-inch waist is like running the Mumbai Marathon in heels. It's impossible! But I've kept a pair of those 24-inch-waist jeans as a souvenir. When I'm sixty and no longer have this figure, it will be a sweet reminder that for one moment in time, everyone wanted to look like me. Although I don't think that has changed too much!

I spent a year being Size Zero. It was a great feeling to begin with: I had wanted that perfect bikini body, and I got my shot right and created a storm, no doubt! It wasn't all great, though. I was being accused of promoting anorexia, other eating disorders I had never even heard of and lord knows

what else. My friends and family had begun to get worried about me because I was losing my famous curves, and slowly becoming uni-dimensional. Every press conference I went to the only questions they'd ask were 'What do you feel about being called Size Zero?' and 'When are you and Saif getting married?' But I live my life on a very simple principle: I have to look at myself in the mirror and love myself first! A whole series of events led to my becoming my ideal size, with the figure that you see on me today.

After seeing me in *Kambakkht Ishq*, Manish Malhotra called Lolo, worried, saying that I was beginning to look too flat-chested. He's one of my dearest friends, my go-to designer, and has been dressing me for years. I trust him and his opinion completely when it comes to clothes and body shape! So hearing that definitely got me thinking.

This was around the time that I began shooting for *3 Idiots* with one of my favourite directors, Raju Hirani. He is one of the most intelligent men I have ever met, and I was in complete awe of him. If he had told me to put on a monkey suit and stand in a corner, I would have done it without asking any questions. One day while we were on sets, he took me aside and gave me an order: 'Gain some weight.' He pointed out that since I had lost so much weight, my face was looking too sharp and angular on screen. Instead of looking like the cute, spontaneous college girl I was supposed to be playing, my face was making me seem harsh and mature. I had no choice but to listen. After all, this was the same man who cast me opposite my favourite actor, Aamir Khan. I owed him.

Saif, who has always been my voice of reason, was also concerned that I had become too thin. Or in his exact words, 'You're looking like a twelve-year-old

Size Zero had changed how I perceived food. This isn't the sort of thing that is temporary.

boy.' He isn't a subtle one! That was it! Two of the most important men in my life at that time wanted me to gain weight. Plus, I had proved my point, shocked enough people and been the cause of one too many debates on skinny vs anorexic. I had made my decision: I was going to put on weight. I made my second big decision regarding my weight: I would become my ideal, perfect size.

So goodbye, Size Zero. It was time to get my curves back.

Luckily, I've been blessed with a nice shape, so a few kilos here and there don't look bad. And I have to confess, putting on weight was fun! I was still eating every two hours, except now I didn't have to limit my portions. Instead of only one slice of pizza, I ate four. My mom was the happiest. She'd been biting her tongue for so long while I was on my mad weight-loss spree that she took it upon herself to single-handedly fatten me up. She started serving butter-soaked parathas for every meal, with my favourite dal and doodhi sabzi to fatten me up.

But that doesn't mean I threw every rule I had learnt until then out of the window. Size Zero had changed how I perceived food. This isn't the sort of thing that is temporary. I was enjoying my food more than ever. I had even begun enjoying vegetables and dishes that I would never have looked at before. I didn't go back to my non-vegetarian ways, because I had seen the dramatic change it had on me, and I had really fallen in love with my new lifestyle. Thankfully, ghar ka khaana is my favourite cuisine.

I rewarded myself with a yummy chocolate cupcake.

Doodhi, karela, lauki: I now love all those weird vegetables that nobody will touch. And yes, I sneaked in a couple of french fries when nobody was looking. Sorry, Rujuta!

From 24 inches, my waistline reached 26 inches and that's when I stopped expanding. My arms and calves, that were lean and mean during my size-zero phase, were now perfectly shapely and lovely. I could fill out a sari like a real Indian diva, and it showed in the way I carried myself. Saif loved my fuller figure, especially my now-recovered butt, which we both agree is my best feature. Like all men, he likes his woman with a little meat on her bones. And I realized that I was happy being curvy.

It's after all my job to look good. An occupational hazard almost! And you can't look good if you don't feel healthy. All it takes is making a few adjustments to your life to make sure it fits in with your lifestyle. For *Halkat jawaani*, my item song in *Heroine*, I wanted to look super toned, so I went back to my *Tashan* diet. Within a few weeks, I had lost four kilos. It's not like I planned to go back to Size Zero, I just wanted to look super-scorching sexy for the song. And of course, I rewarded myself for the hard work with a yummy chocolate cupcake the day the shoot was over!

The key is to embrace this eating cycle completely. I have become the best judge of what my body needs. It's almost like my brain has turned into an alarm clock, so I know I need to have my mango milkshake in the next 15 minutes, without my stomach

It's almost like my brain has turned into an alarm clock, so I know I need to have my mango milkshake in the next 15 minutes.

growling to announce that it's hungry. But just because I'm on a diet doesn't mean I won't go out to dinner with my friends. I just make sure I eat on time, even if it means having to call ahead to inform the hosts of my schedule.

This rollercoaster ride of losing my baby fat, becoming super skinny and now being sexy and curvy has taught me one thing: looking great is 40 per cent style and 60 per cent confidence. It used to be a daily battle between me and those parts of my body that I didn't think were perfect. But I'm no longer

shy about showing them off. In fact, I'm often the one forcing Lolo who has an amazing figure to dress more daringly. When we were both walking the ramp for Salman's Being Human show at HDIL India Couture Week, she needed some convincing to wear the colourful sleeveless ganjis. And I? I just threw mine on and decided I was going to rock it.

I'm not going to wear a bikini on screen again: frankly, I don't have the mindset for it now. But I still ask my stylist to get me some of the most daring backless gowns

I'm not a fan of the weighing scale.

for a red-carpet premiere, even if I'm no longer Size Zero. And all my fans agree that they like this Bebo better. The secret is to accept your flaws, because often those are the parts which make you stand out from a crowd. Once you begin to love your flaws, you can turn them into plus points.

And of course, work on making the other parts look good. It took me a while to zone in on my ideal figure and body. But when I saw myself on screen in a red sari, I knew *Chammak Challo* is for me!

I have also realized that more than thin or fat, it's all about figuring out your ideal weight and size. You need to figure this one out for yourself. I have gone through my phases; the great part is I loved myself in all shapes and avatars! Begin with loving your body, stretch marks and all.

I'm not a fan of the weighing scale. For me weight is a more visual and physical experience. Just remember, ladies, it's great to be thin, but it's sexy to be voluptuous and even sexier to be able to carry it all off with oodles of confidence.

GETTING RID OF EXCESS BAGGAGE

THE DIET PLAN!

My size-zero 'phase' was more than a phase. I had learnt to respect food, fitness and most of all my body. In that sense it changed my life. It changed my perception of food, exercise and health completely, and I hope forever. I did not want to go back to being careless and reckless when it came to my body. Being on a strict diet had done more than just help me lose weight. It had taught me how to lead a fit and fabulous life!

Earlier I had cringed at the very word diet. There was something so clinical about the whole thing. And trust me, if I had to make a choice between being thin and being happy, I'd probably be a chubby chica my entire life. I've dieted, exercised and worked really hard to have a good figure, but if it came at the cost of living a normal life, I'd give it up in a second. The biggest misconception about eating right that most people have is that you have to sacrifice all the yummy food that you love. Not true.

Rujuta ensured that I did not have to give up my parathas, paneer and cheese! She had me eating all the time but she had me eating right and balancing my food and quantity of food right. The art of juggling and balance is the key to a good diet plan. So remember, don't starve yourself or fall for the ridiculous number of fad diets out there and instead ask yourself the following questions:

THE DIET PLAN!

What should I be eating? When should I be eating? How frequently should I be eating? And, how much is the right amount of food I should be eating? Once you start asking the right questions you then begin understanding food and your body! And apart from all of this don't let your eating habits take the joy of eating away from you. Rujuta made me understand the importance of understanding and relishing my food.

From the start I knew I had to be a normal functioning human being. There were certain things I just refused to compromise on. I need to start my day with a cup of hot steaming chai. I can't even think straight without it. It's a habit I've inherited from my grandmother, and just like her I love my tea with jam sandwiches and biscuits. Even though Rujuta has banned coffee

and tea from all her clients' diets, she knows that it's impossible for me to survive without my daily dose. So we struck a bargain and I have my morning cup of tea till date . . . but only after I eat a fruit.

The same goes for sweets. I don't have sugar cravings but imagine all your friends sitting down to gorge on some mouth-watering gajar ka halwa while you just watch them and curse silently. No way! I'll have a tiny bit to satisfy my taste-buds, but I won't go overboard with my helping. And since my staff know how much I like home-cooked food, they keep bringing me delicious tiffins filled with goodies made with love by their moms. They also take care to keep my diet restrictions in mind, and won't send anything which is overloaded with oil or ghee. Since they love surprising me

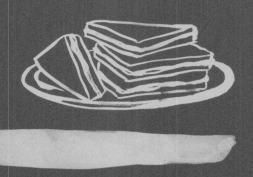

And that's the only way you'll ever be motivated to get fit: when you're unhappy with the way you look and feel, and decide to take responsibility for it.

Being fit and healthy should not be an option. Not if you want to really enjoy your life, have a great personality and look good in whatever you wear. You should get fit! But being fit doesn't mean being boring or turning your back on all the pleasures of life. You just need to find the right balance, and have patience with yourself when you make mistakes. If a round little Punjabi girl like me who loved mutton biryani can now have a 26-inch waist and eat doodhi sabzi with equal relish instead, there's nothing stopping you.

I did outgrow my size-zero phase, but for those who want to lose those extra kilos, I would definitely recommend it but if and only if you consult the right dietician and fitness specialist. At the end of the day, your health is everything so if you plan on losing weight, do it the right way: like I did! I have charted out my fitness and diet schedule so you know exactly how I maintain my weight and shape today. And starvation is not the answer. The right combination of food, exercise and plain old determination that you can do it is what will get you to lose those extra kilos and become your ideal size, whatever that is: Size 0 or Size 12!

with my favourite dishes, I never have to even think of ordering in. It's like I've started my own Kareena catering service!

Going on a diet isn't about denying yourself food. It's about understanding your food and custom-creating a diet which will suit you, keeping in mind the basic principles of health and nutrition. Enjoying everything in moderation is my key to health and happiness. Oh, and throwing out the weighing scale. I don't believe in standing on a machine every morning and allowing it to tell you whether you're fit or fat. You can judge that for yourself. When you look into the mirror and see tummy tyres hanging everywhere, or you can't climb three flights of stairs without huffing and puffing, or you can't fit into your favourite pair of jeans anymore, you know you're not in the best shape.

The 3-step get-ready agenda

1. CREATE YOUR OWN GOAL

I have been in and out of gyms, lost a kilo here and gained a kilo there and been totally non-committal about my weight for the longest time. Coz it didn't really matter. But when I had to get my Bikini Body ready, I found a new goal for myself. I wanted to become super thin. Maybe it was because I wanted to shock and scandalize the industry. Or maybe it was because my director told me to get ready for the shot! Or maybe I just wanted to know what it would feel like to have my Ursula Andress moment. All I know is I was super determined and sure about the fact that I was going to do this. Today, I might be over my size-zero days but I have a new goal in mind: to stay my curvy shapely self and have that perfect body! And nothing works like self-motivation. So think about it seriously. Make your decision, set your target and remind yourself of it every single day! If you want a constant reminder, scribble it on Post-its and stick it on your refrigerator, work desk or even your bathroom mirror.

2. GET YOUR SUPPORT SYSTEM TOGETHER

This is not an easy process. When everyday stress catches up, you might be tempted to binge or sleep through your exercise hour. You need to keep yourself motivated but more importantly you need to have people whom you can rely on for unbiased support, advice and love. And this is probably the time you need your 4

a.m. friend the most! Create your own team of friends, professionals and family to help keep you motivated. Size Zero would never have happened if it wasn't for my support system: my mother, sister, Saif, Rujuta, Payal, even Prakash, my assistant and right-hand man, who made sure my meals would appear on time, even if we were by a lake in Ladakh. He carries a copy of my diet schedule everywhere we go. But you can't have Prakash—he's all mine!

3. GET INVOLVED

You definitely need to equip yourself with a good dietician and fitness trainer. You need someone you can refer to not just for a diet plan or a workout schedule but also to work with you through your problems. Everybody is different and needs personal attention and space. I call myself Rujuta's assistant, because I've become a part-time nutritionist for anyone who'll listen. We prepare my diets together, which makes it easier for me to stick to the plan. Knowing what foods are good for you and what doesn't work also allows you to improvise on the go. Even with exercise, I had to find my niche. The gym wasn't for me but yoga is! It has transformed my life. It's as much an exercise routine as it is a stress-buster for me. Today, I understand each asana and can create my own workouts to suit my body. Remember, to get into shape you need to have the right diet and fitness regime in place. Figure out what works for you. And then plunge yourself into that and understand it inside out!

Diet Dos and Don'ts

- **DO** eat something within the first 10 minutes of waking up. **DON'T** start your day with tea or coffee.

- **DO** try and eat as much home-cooked food as possible and plan your 6 p.m. meal well in advance. **DON'T** leave everything to chance, because you'll probably land up eating junk food by 6 p.m.

- **DO** make exercise an integral part of your life. Think of things outside of the gym which can become a workout. So go dancing, play a sport, run or go for a brisk walk in the park with your girlfriends. **DON'T** bother about counting calories; it will only depress you and take the joy out of eating.

- **DO** include good fats in your daily meals: they keep your body young and healthy. Ghee, peanuts, cheese and paneer are considered to be essential fats. **DON'T** give in to junk food cravings.

- **DO** embrace all kinds of food, even those which are not traditionally considered healthy, like gulab jamuns and samosas. **DON'T** berate yourself for eating one extra scoop of ice cream. Just plan your indulgences so that you remain in control.

- **DO** eat according to your appetite. That is based on how much physical and mental labour you put into your day, and the kinds of energy required to finish your tasks properly. **DON'T** standardize portions because your energy output changes every day.

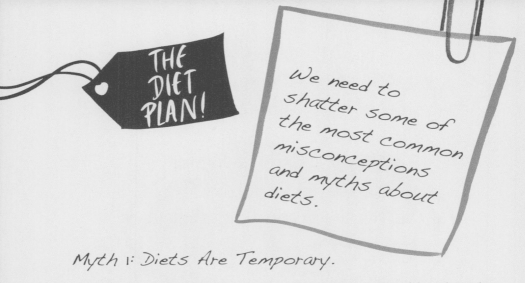

We need to shatter some of the most common misconceptions and myths about diets.

Myth 1: Diets Are Temporary.

Unfortunately, this is the biggest myth that exists. Your diet is what and how much you eat every day for the rest of your life. If you are a fan of fad diets, the truth is you're only harming your body! So, you will lose some weight for some time, and before you know it you're back where you started. To lose and maintain your weight over a period of time you need to understand and eat right every single day. To begin with, make your dietician your friend and design a food plan that you can permanently absorb into your life. Begin by understanding food and the various food groups. So you can improvise whenever required. Also, keep in mind your lifestyle and your likes and dislikes. Making small changes every now and then, depending on where you live, your daily routine, travelling schedules etc. helps make your diet easy to follow and prevents boredom. You even need to adapt your eating habits to the climate, because your body requires different nutrition depending on how hot or cold the weather is. Soups keep you warm in the winter, while fresh vegetable and fruit juices keep your body going in the summer. You need to make up your mind, learn about food and understand what you're putting into your mouth. It's the easiest thing to do once you begin. Trust me on this one! The only thing standing between you and the body you deserve is a wrong mindset.

Myth 2: A Diet Is Based on Measured Portions.

Diets based on measured portions cannot and will not work. Everybody is different. Our lifestyles are different and our pace of work is different. The one-diet-suits-all formula cannot be effective ever. But there is a simple formula you can keep in mind: match your input to your output! So, change your food portion size according to the level of activity you have that day. Standard portions don't work, because your routine changes and you might need more energy sometimes. Of course, you shouldn't use that as an excuse to eat a kilo of cake, when you know a slice is all you really need.

Myth 3: Don't Live to Eat. Eat to Live!

I say, enjoy your food! Relish and cherish your food. I love my food and will continue to do so. The only way I know how to lose weight is by eating. But instead of getting caught up in calorie counting, I make sure to balance the nutrients in my meal with calories. If my friend's mother makes me some mithai, there's no saying no. I just eat enough of veggies and fruits to give my body enough fibre to digest the sugar and butter quickly. Dieting doesn't have to be dramatic. We have Bollywood movies for that.

Swap your sugar-heavy milk chocolate for a small piece of pure dark chocolate to satisfy that craving.

Myth 4: Cut the Carbs and You Cut the Fat.

If Rujuta had told me I couldn't eat parathas anymore, I would have walked out on her on day one. The key is not to cut any food group out of your diet, because they all have important roles to play in keeping your body in top shape. The key is to differentiate between good carbs and bad carbs, or essential fat from useless fat, and then you won't be denying your body the treatment it deserves. Brown bread and wholegrain parathas are good carbs, because they're packed with nutrients, and take longer to break down. Peanuts are loaded with fatty oils, but these keep your skin looking fresh and young. Educate yourself about the food you eat and that will make dieting easier.

Myth 5: Cheat Days Are Allowed!

Diet during the week and indulge over the weekend. This is the cheat sheet that most dieters follow. Effectively you lose kilos only to gain them over the weekend. But the biggest flaw is that you've still not changed your perception of food. It's not about denying yourself what you love to eat, but about finding healthier alternatives so that you can permanently change your lifestyle. If you have a sweet tooth, try munching on fresh or dry fruits instead of tiramisu. Or swapping your sugar-heavy milk chocolate for a small piece of pure dark chocolate to satisfy that craving. Keep your body happy with the kind of food it craves instead of waiting for the weekend to throw it all away.

MY DAILY DIET PLAN

I've torn a page off my daily diet plan, to give you an idea of how to plan your own.

BEBO'S FOOD DIARY • MUMBAI • 4 JUNE 2011

Meal Timing	Food/Menu	Supplements
Meal One On rising (9 a.m.)	Banana or any fresh fruit	Vitamin B complex
Meal Two 11 a.m.	Idli + chutney + sambar or poha	Vitamin C + E
Meal Three 1 p.m.	Wholewheat roti + seasonal vegetable (sabzi) + yogurt	
Meal Four 3 p.m.	Peanuts or foxnuts (makhana)	Evening primrose oil
Meal Five 5 p.m.	Cherries/gooseberries	
Meal Six 7 p.m.	Soya milk or cheese or fruit yogurt	
Meal Seven 9.30 p.m.	Dal + vegetable pulao + yogurt	Antioxidant
Bedtime		Calcium citrate

Here's another one of my diet plans but from my size-zero days.

BEBO'S FOOD DIARY • LADAKH • 12 SEPT 2008

Meal Timing	Food/Menu	Supplements
Meal One On rising (7 a.m.)	Papaya or any fresh fruit	Vitamin B complex
Meal Two 8.30 a.m.	Muesli + milk or wholewheat bread/toast + sea buckthorn jam	Vitamin C + E
Meal Three 11.30 a.m.	Fresh pear or apple	
Meal Four 1.30 p.m.	Momos + chutney/thukpa	Evening primrose oil
Meal Five 4.30 p.m.	Slice of cow cheese or goat cheese	
Meal Six 6.30 p.m.	Thukpa with veggies	
Meal Seven 8 p.m.	Tofu/cottage cheese stir fry + 1 piece of garlic bread + Grilled veggies + tomato soup	Antioxidant
Bedtime		Calcium citrate
If hungry	Glass of skimmed milk	

MY DAILY DIET PLAN

Some pointers to keep in mind when creating your diet plan:

- My size-zero diet had me eating every two hours and as you can see I continue to do so. A standard diet should be **a minimum of five meals a day**. Staying hungry is never the answer. You need to eat but you also need to eat right. If you eat through the day, you avoid hunger pangs and bingeing. You also give your body enough time to digest the food properly.

- If you go through my diet plan, you will realize it's like anybody's daily food routine. The big difference is in what I'm eating in between the big meals. **Remember to keep your snacks healthy**; try and stick to fruits, nuts, yogurt, cheese and milk. This is usually where we slip up on a day-to-day basis.

- Ensure that you **cover all the food groups through the day**, so you have your share of protein, carbohydrate, fats and sugars, fibre and dairy. Educate yourself on what food comes under which food group and make a list of good and bad foods keeping in mind your likes and dislikes. Keep your breakfast, lunch and dinner balanced and ensure that you get enough of all the food groups.

- Make your diet plan as **practical and user-friendly** as you can. Plan your meals in advance and take into account the accessibility and availability of food. I have purposely chosen my Ladakh diet plan so you get an idea of how to customize your diet when you're not at home. Work with local food when you're travelling.

- **Stay hydrated throughout**. You need a minimum of 5 litres of water per day. And at least two to three cups of either mint tea or green tea or the like. You have tons of options today from tulsi and jasmine to chamomile and white tea, to name a few. You can also add fresh fruit or vegetable juices, and milk shakes.

- Make sure you **take your supplements**. As you can see from the plan there's a whole host of supplements to keep my nutritional balance in check. Don't fall for the multi-vitamin scam. You need your body well-nourished with all the adequate minerals and vitamins which come from a variety of sources. I make sure I have my Vitamin E supplement every alternate day.

- Make a list of **healthy and easy-to-carry snacks** for when you feel peckish between meals. I personally love peanuts, channa, fruits and buttermilk; and when I was in Ladakh, I had butter tea (ladakhi chai) which was delicious!

- And, of course eat ghar ka khana as much as you can. Don't clutter your everyday diet with too much junk food. Or, you could **turn your guilty pleasure into good food**. I'm addicted to chilli cheese toast, so I found a way to make it as healthy as possible. A slice of toasted brown or wholegrain bread, topped with one slice of cheese and a few chilli flakes—no butter, no oil and no white bread. It has all the flavour of fast food, but is packed with good carbs, protein and calcium.At the same time, don't forget to satisfy your cravings, but don't be a glutton. If I'm craving chocolate cake, I'll cut a thin slice to make me happy. And I don't suffer from calorie guilt afterwards.

- Most importantly, **don't gobble your food**. Chew and relish it. Take your time over your meal. It takes time for the brain to register that your tummy is full and when we pack it in quickly, the signal is delayed and we're over-eating!

- If you compare the two diet plans, you will notice they are almost the same in terms of meal timings and the food groups covered in each meal. The **ONLY** difference in my diet during my size-zero days and today is in the quantity of food. So, **if you want to lose more weight, you cut down on your portions and when you want to lose less weight you increase your portions**. So trust your judgement here; of course, you shouldn't overdo the portions either. Learn to listen to your body. In a few days of working with this diet you will figure out how your body responds to the various portions. Eating every two hours helps you balance portions immediately. And remember my little secret: **moderation**!

The Five Super Foods

If you haven't already included these five diet must-haves into your daily routine, fill your kitchen cabinets with them now.

PEANUTS Cheap and available throughout the year, this is one action-packed nut! They are high in Vitamin B, protein and essential fats. Eat them as a mid-meal snack and you'll discover smoother skin.

YOGURT/DAHI Not only is yogurt high in calcium which is good for your bones, but it is also rich in B12, and works miracles for warding off acne. It also gives your skin a well-hydrated look.

SINGLE POLISHED RICE Unlike white rice which has been robbed of all the nutrients, single polished rice is jam-packed with essential amino acids, fibre and carbs which combat wrinkles.

HOME-MADE GHEE You might be looking at me in shock, but trust me. This is the ultimate weapon in hydration and lubrication, and will ensure that your skin looks good, feels great and remains healthy.

SEASONAL FRUITS I cannot tell you enough how important fruits are in any diet. Mangoes, bananas, chickoos, custard apple (seetaphal), avocado and grapes are loaded with nutrients, phytochemicals and microminerals. You should not go a single day without fruits if you can help it, since they also nourish the delicate skin under the eyes.

THE QUEEN OF SURYA NAMASKARS!

When it comes to everyday fitness, you need to be doing something to begin with. Coz a diet alone doesn't make you healthy and your body shapely. You have to work on your body, even to get the curves right! I'm a big believer in brisk outdoor walks, especially if you're lucky enough to have a park, beach or boulevard near your house. If yoga isn't your cup of tea, try pilates, zoomba or cardio; you could even go for a run, box, swim, play a sport or get yourself a skipping rope! The options are endless. It took me a while to find something I could work with. Yoga and I have had a tumultuous relationship. The first time I tried it, I hated it. Today I am a self-declared addict! And I have to thank Payal for that.

Payal had realized that anything monotonous and boring wouldn't work with me. Remember I had already quit once and, with my history with gymming, she perfectly understood that routine doesn't work for me. So she devised a yoga fitness routine, which was hectic, energetic and different each time we tried it. A couple of asanas were of course repetitive but only the ones I grew super fond of.

The surya namaskar and I have a strange story. When we began I just couldn't get it right. It became a sort of challenge, so I kept at it. It grew into a sort of obsession; I had to get it right. I went on to master it to such a degree that Payal has nicknamed me queen of the surya namaskars, because now I can do about 108 without a break. It is my absolute favourite asana and Payal cleverly worked that in whenever I was on the verge of giving up on some

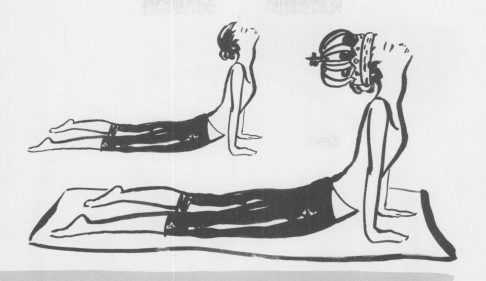

impossible asana. The whole challenge behind getting an asana right became a driving force in my workout routine. Twinkle, another one from my army of yoga gurus trained by Payal, helped me overcome my vertigo by encouraging me to do headstands. The first time she suggested it, I was terrified. But she didn't give up, so neither could I.

I do improvise on my workouts a lot more now. Yoga has made me calmer and more in control of my life than ever before. It transforms the mind, which in turn, helps in making the best body. It has helped me grow and mature. Friends and family tell me they've noticed a complete change in my aura. I never miss a class, except when I'm travelling. And even then, I spend at least 45 minutes doing the asanas on my own. And this is one of the best things about yoga: you don't need any fancy equipment or anything; all you need is to know your asanas. In fact, I never compromise on my early morning yoga sessions. Even my directors try and juggle shoot schedules around to accommodate them. Fresh air, bright sunshine and an hour of tough asanas: that's the perfect start to my day.

My size-zero yoga routine was one hour a day, five days a week for a period of ten months. And this hasn't changed a bit. Even though I'm more flexible with my diet now I still do my yoga every day. I'm completely hooked. It is a life-changing way of exercising and I would whole-heartedly recommend it to you. And the best part of it is it isn't boring! So here's a lowdown of my yoga schedule, my favourite asanas and tons of tips that I have picked up along the way.

5 STEPS TO GETTING YOGA-READY

STEP 1: FIND YOUR STYLE

Do a bit of research on the various kinds of yoga classes available. I recommend Bharat Thakur wholeheartedly! But try a couple of different styles to see which suits you.

STEP 2: IN CLASS OR AT HOME?

You need to get the asanas right and be able to do it accurately. You don't want it causing you more harm than good. So you need a good trainer! Your big decision is if you want to work out with other people in a yoga studio or at home with a personal trainer. I suggest you consider both and weigh the pros and cons of each and see what suits you best.

Shortlist the yoga courses offered close by. If you're enrolling in a class make sure it's either close to your office or your home. You don't want to be stuck in traffic and give yourself another excuse to quit!

There's also the option of getting yourself a personal trainer. Which is great coz they will work on your body one-on-one and can customize your workout for you.

5 STEPS TO GETTING YOGA-READY

STEP 3: TIME IT RIGHT

Figure out your workout timings. This is the most crucial. You need to block those one or two hours every day. If you're a morning person like me, sign up for a class that begins at 6 a.m. or whatever time you wake up. If evenings suit you better, make sure you plan it at such a time that if there's a night-out plan or a delayed meeting, you don't give it a miss. Schedule this into your calendar and for at least the first month, don't miss a single class.

STEP 4: GEAR UP

Once you've signed on, get yourself the right yoga gear. The essentials include:

- Since yoga is done the floor, you need to protect your back. Buying a **yoga mat** which not only gives your spine a little cushioning, but also offers better grip is a good option. Pick a happy colour that will motivate you to work harder. Adidas makes great yoga mats, and Sivakasi offers a lovely variety.
- The right clothes are very important because so much of yoga is about stretching and contorting your body. I switch between **track pants** from

Sweaty Betty in London and **cotton pyjamas**, though lots of people prefer wearing shorts. Wearing a loose shirt might become a problem when you are in a downward asana, so something more clingy like a ganji works better!
- Get yourself **good innerwear**. You definitely need a well-fitting sports bra for added support.

STEP 5: YOGA 101

Know the basics before you begin. Now that you're all signed up, here's what you need to keep in mind when you begin your yoga workout:

- Never work out on a full stomach. If you work out after breakfast, wait for two hours. Heavier meals require a gap of at least four hours.
- When you start yoga, you might feel dizzy in the beginning. This is common with people who don't exercise regularly. Don't panic: it's normal and it will get better.
- It's important to rehydrate yourself. Drink at least four to five litres of water a day.
- Take a break of at least 10 seconds between each asana in the sequence.
- Stretch before and after the workout, even if only for a few minutes.

MY DAILY YOGA WORKOUT

Here's a sample daily workout from my usual yoga regime. Of course, I do mix it up quite a bit. And keep changing around the order of the asanas or even try different asanas.

1. Warm-Up

Every workout, even yoga, must begin with a warm-up to open up the muscles. I used to start every yoga session with about 5 to 6 minutes of warm-up exercises like dynamic stretches. Breathing is the most important part of yoga, so you must learn to control your breathing to optimize your workout.

2. The Surya Namaskar (25 Rounds)

The surya namaskar targets every muscle in the body. Be ready to be completely out of breath, especially if you're new to yoga. For a first-timer, it might be better if you stick to five surya namaskars to begin with. Here's a little tip that helped me master this asana: let each step be determined by your breath. Inhale and exhale your way through this and you will pick it up in no time. Also, once your body is fitter it stops hurting and feels wonderful!

• Join your palms together in front of your chest as you stand. • As you inhale deeply, stretch your arms up to the sky, chin up. • Exhale as you bend fully at the waist, fingers touching your toes. • Inhale, and stretch your right foot back, and then the left, so that you are balancing on your hands and feet. • Exhale as you drop your head between your hands.• Inhale as you stretch your body upward, so that your hips are resting on the floor, while your torso and face are turned upwards. • Exhale and reverse the pose into a pyramid shape, face touching the floor and hips up. Bring your right foot forward, then the left, till you are once again bending at the waist with your feet together. • Inhale as you lift up, and go back to the starting position.

We'd continue with a full body workout, comprising mainly standing postures. This is usually the most hectic part of the workout.

CHAKRASANA (ONE SET)

• Lie on your back, with your knees bent and your feet near your hips. • Place your palms by your shoulders, elbows bent, and fingers facing in the direction of your head. • Inhale and slowly raise your body upward, so that your weight rests on your feet and palms, resulting in the curving of your spine. • Retain the pose for a few seconds, then exhaling normally, lower the body back into shavasana.

ARDHACHANDRASANAS (ONE SET)

• Start with trikonasana, putting your right hand on your hip. • Bend your right knee gently, moving forward. • Move your right hand forward, pushing it a few inches ahead of the toes of your right leg. Exhale as you keep your right hand and right heel on the floor for balance. • Lift your left leg parallel to the floor. • Lift your left hand to align with your right hand.

TRIKONASANA (ONE SET)

• Stand straight with legs together and hands by the side of the thighs. • Slowly move your legs apart at a distance of 2 to 3 feet raising both hands sideways at shoulder level with your palms facing the floor. • Then slowly bend forward towards the right side touching the big toe of the right leg with the left hand without bending your knees. • Raise your right hand up and look up towards the right hand, breathing normally.• Hold this for some time and come back to the starting position. • Repeat on the other side.

PADHASTASANA
(HOLD FOR 30 SECONDS)
• Get into the tala asana position, where your arms are extended above your head. • Exhale and bend forward at the hips, till your upper torso and arms are hanging straight down beside your legs. • Inhale slowly, as you look up, lengthening the spine. • Exhale, relax the head, neck and spine downwards, fixing your fingers and palms firmly under your toes. • Then release your hands and straighten your arms. • Inhale and slowly come back up into tala asana. • Exhale as you lower your hands and relax.

VRIKSHASANA
(ONE SET)
• Stand with your feet together, arms on either side. • Lift your right leg and fold it at the knee. • Then hold the ankle with both hands and pull your leg up, resting your foot on the upper part of your left thigh, toes pointing downwards. • As you balance on your left leg, join your palms in front of your chest. • Inhale slowly as you raise both hands above your head, arms slightly bent. • Stretch your hands and body up as you gaze ahead. • Slowly return to the standing position.

After you're completely out of breath, you'll be begging to sit down. Lucky for you, yoga also has a number of asanas that can be performed in the sitting position.

USTRASANA (ONE SET)
• Sit with your legs folded under you, bottom balanced on the soles of your feet in vajrasana. • Raise your body so that you are kneeling, and raise your hands over your head as you inhale. • Slowly bend backwards, and hold the right heel and then the left with corresponding hands. Exhale as you arch the spine and neck, pushing your pelvis forward. • Hold for four counts before you return to the starting position.

BHADRASANA (ONE SET)
• Sit with your legs spread out, then bring them together so that the soles are touching. • Draw the heels as close to the body as possible. • Try to touch your knees to the floor on either side, as your neck remains straight and your abdomen is sucked in. • Use butterfly movements: moving the knees up and down slowly. This improves flexibility.

JANUSHIRASANA (ONE SET)
• Sit straight, legs stretched forward. • Bend your right leg so that the sole is against the right thigh. • Press the perineum with the heel. • Inhale as you raise both the hands over your head. • Exhale as you bend forward, trying to touch the left knee with your forehead. • Holding the left toe with your right hand, let your left hand rest on your back. • Your right elbow should touch the ground. • Inhale as you return to the normal position, and repeat on the other side.

VAKRASANA (ONE SET)
• As you sit, stretch out your legs, then raise the right leg by bending the knee. • Pull your foot towards you till it rests beside your left knee. • Keeping your right hand behind the back, bring your left arm over your right knee and hold your right ankle. • Then push your right knee to the left as far as possible. • Exhale as you twist your torso to the right, using your left arm for support. • Look towards the right shoulder. • Repeat on the other side.

ARDHAMATSYENDRASANA (ONE SET)
• Sit with your legs folded under you, toes facing outward. • Slowly shift your weight to the right so that your bottom touches the ground. • Bring your left leg over your right, placing the foot against the outside of the right knee. • Bring your right heel in close to your bottom, keeping the spine erect. • Stretch your arms out to the sides at shoulder level, and twist your body to the left. • Bringing your right arm down against the outside of your left knee, hold your foot with your right hand, and place your left hand on the floor behind you. • As you exhale, twist as far as possible to the left, looking over the left shoulder.

5. Full Body Workout (In Supine Position)

By this stage, you'll give anything to just crawl back into bed and pass out. But take a deep breath, like a true yogic master and begin with the asanas conducted in the supine position.

SHAVASANA OR DEEP BREATHING (FOR 2 MINUTES)
• Lie flat on your back, feet spreadeagled and arms about 6 inches away from the body. • Keep your palms relaxed and facing upwards. • As you close your eyes, relax the muscles in your feet, then knees, chest, arms, and finally, your head. • Concentrate on your breathing, which should be slow and effortless. • Hold for 10 seconds.

SUPTATADASANA (ONE SET)
• Begin by lying on your back, arms stretched past your head. • As you lift your hips off the floor inhaling, bring your legs up, over and beyond your head, till they touch the floor. • Lifting your back as far as possible move your legs forward, so that your spine is completely stretched. • Place your hands on your back, as high as possible, elbows on the floor. • Push your back upwards with your hands. • Rest your weight on your shoulders. • Lift up your legs, one at a time, so that your pelvis and legs are in a straight line. • Hold as you try to balance this. • Slowly bring your legs back to the mat, one by one, and stretch out your arms away from you.

UTTANPADASANA (ONE SET)
• Lie on your back, legs extended and your feet together. • Your palms should be touching the sides of your body and facing down. • Inhale as you raise your legs slowly, first to 30 degrees, then 60, till you hit 90. • Pause at each angle, but don't bend your knees. • Hold this position with your toes pointed upwards. • Exhale as you return the same way to the first position.

SARAL MATSYASANA (ONE SET)
• Lie on your back, feet and arms straight. • Place your hands, palms downwards, beneath the thighs so that you are resting on them. • Bend the elbows and raise your chest and head. • Drop your head backwards so that the top of your head is touching the ground. • Your weight should be balanced on the elbows. • Hold as you breathe normally. • Lower your head and unfurl your back to return to shavasana.

ARDHAPAWANMUKTASANA (ONE SET)
• Lie on your back with your feet together, palms placed beside the body. • Inhale as you raise your right leg and bend it at the knee. • Bring your thigh towards your abdomen, interlock your fingers behind it and exhaling press the thigh against the abdomen. • Inhale as you stretch your leg up, then exhale as you bring your leg back to the floor. • Repeat with your left leg.

PAWANMUKTASANA (ONE SET)
• Lie on your back with your hands by your side. • Inhale as you raise both your legs to 90 degrees, and bend them at the knees. • Lock your fingers behind your legs, a little below the knees. • Exhale as you bring your thighs towards your chest by contracting the abdominal muscles. • Hold for a few seconds, before returning to the original position, in reverse, as Ardha Pavan Muktasana.

SETUBHANDHASANA (ONE SET)
• Begin in Shavasana, then raise your knees so that your feet are close to your hips, keeping them apart.

• Your hands should rest near your thighs. • As you inhale, raise your hips and hands simultaneously. • Bring your hands over your head till they are resting on the floor. • Exhale, and bring your hands and hips back to the starting position.

NAUKASANA (THREE SETS)
• Lie down on your back with your feet together and your palms resting on your thighs. • Inhale and raise both legs up, then raise the upper body off the floor. • Hold it for some time while breathing normally keeping your hands parallel to the floor. • Slowly come back to the starting position.

6. Chant and Unwind!

This was undoubtedly my favourite part of the workout. By the end of it your body has been stretched to its maximum and you're ready to quit. The brief chanting and meditative quality of letting your body unwind just makes you feel completely revitalized when you open your eyes again!

Relax with your eyes closed for about 2 minutes. Chant Om and let your body rest.

My Favourite Yoga Asanas

Here's a list of my favourite asanas; you can try different permutations and combinations to give a nice variety to your workout. Work with the asanas, and figure out your favourites. It will make your workout a lot more interesting.

SURYA NAMASKAR (THE SUN SALUTATION)

As mentioned earlier this is a complete workout in itself. If you've been a cardio freak, you'll love this. It also helps balance and posture, and keeps all the joints, muscles and internal organs stimulated and balanced. It's ideal for people with busy schedules.

TRIKONASANA (THE TRIANGLE POSE)

Forget about crunches and sit-ups. This pose works well to target the muscles around the waist and in your legs, and keeps your spine supple. It will also improve your appetite and digestion.

NATARAJASANA (LORD SHIVA'S POSE)

A calming asana, this pose balances the nervous system, and helps improve flexibility in the legs. • Stand with your left leg straight and your right folded back. • Inhale as you grip your right leg with your right hand, then exhale. • Inhale and raise your left arm alongside the ear. • Stretch your right heel away from your body, while maintaining the weight on your left foot. • Slowly bend forward till the chest and arm become parallel to the floor and your knee, thigh, hip, spine and arm are in a straight line.

SARVANGASANA (THE SHOULDER STAND)

If you have puffy bags under the eyes like me, this is the pose that will give you some relief. It also helps stimulate hair growth, as the inverted pose improves blood circulation. • Lie on your back, arms straight down by your sides. • As you inhale, contract your stomach muscles and swing your legs upwards at a 90 degree angle to your body. • Using your arms as a support, raise your waist off the floor, bending your legs forward till they reach just past your head. • Inhale as you raise your back, and place your hands against the upper back for support. • Your chin should be pressed against your chest, creating a chin lock. • Breathe normally.

HALASANA (THE PLOUGH OR WHEELBARROW POSE)

This is a tough one, and requires more strength than the others. But once you've mastered it, you will be relieved of any backaches and stomach pains. It's also great for losing weight. • From the sarvangasana, exhale as you bend your hip to lower your feet to the floor, over and behind your head. • Push your bottom up as far as possible, drawing your groin inward. • Stretch your arms out behind you, in the opposite direction of the legs. • Clasp your fingers together, and use the arms as support. • Bring your hands flat on the floor for support to go back to sarvangasana.

CHAKRASANA (THE WHEEL POSE)

This asana is tailor-made for women, and helps to improve overall digestion and breathing.

HANUMANASANA (THE MONKEY POSE)

Get the full benefit of a treadmill workout with this pose which targets and tones the leg muscles, my problem area. • Begin by kneeling on the floor. Place your right foot about a foot in front of your left knee, and rotate your right thigh outward. Exhale as you lean forward, pushing your weight on to your palms which are resting on the floor. • Slowly slide your left knee back, straightening the knee. • Now, let your right thigh straighten out in front of you. • Make sure your right knee points directly upwards, and your back leg extends straight, not angled. Stretch your arms straight up towards the ceiling. • Then, press your hands to the floor, turn the front leg out slightly as you return to your starting position.

Make Your Workout Work for You

I know how difficult it is to stick to a workout regime. So here are a few things I did to make my workout work for me.

- If you get bored easily and are anything like me, try and get plenty of fresh air when you exercise. I worked out for years in an air-conditioned gym and it didn't help me much. I'd love to have a big balcony where I could practice all my asanas, but I have to make do with opening the windows and setting up my mat in the sun. Make your environment work for you. If gymming is your thing, make yourself that perfect playlist on your iPod. If it's running, find yourself a beautiful park. If you like working out at home, beautify your exercise corner.

- Don't get depressed if you have skinny calves or back fat or fat ankles; just camouflage them. We all have parts we'd like to change. The key is to focus on the part of your body that you like the most, and highlight that by exercising and dressing well. There was a time when I'd have happily given one big fat movie cheque to lose all my weight. But don't go overboard. Stay focused on building your assets and working with your flaws. This will help you appreciate your body which is the biggest motivator!

- Get a partner to exercise with you. I enjoy working out a lot more when I have company. Plus they keep me motivated. I have managed to convince Lolo, Amrita and Saif to quit the gym and try yoga instead. Whenever Saif is not shooting, he joins my yoga session. So now I have company too! Get your best friend, boyfriend or husband to keep you company. You'll both be fitter and happier.

Happy Working Out!

DELHI

HONG KONG

MUMBAI

BANGKOK

JET~SET

After all that working out, I think we need to take a break! Phew! You know what my favourite part of going to school as a kid was? The holidays! When we were younger, taking a family vacation meant no curfews, no homework and as much exciting foreign junk food as I could swallow without exploding. And don't think we were pampered brats flying first class. My parents only travelled economy, because my lovely middle-class mom was determined not to spoil her daughters.

My first memory of travelling abroad was going to Hong Kong with both my parents. I must have been five years old, but I remember Lolo and I were dazzled by the lights and sounds of this big new city. And since my whole family loves Chinese food, this was paradise. We spent more time eating than we did sightseeing. And though I don't travel to South-East Asia very often now, I remember the people there as being warm and friendly.

Over the years, I've become a seasoned traveller, although I'm still quite a novice when it comes to trains! I have taken a train ride on my own, though I'll admit it was a complete disaster. Studying in Welham Girls in Dehradun, I was the only girl in my class who'd fly home for the holidays, while all my classmates and friends went to Delhi by bus and caught the Rajdhani home. So I fought with my mom and told her, 'I want to take the train too.' Bad idea. It was the worst journey ever! I even got sick because

NEW YORK CITY

LONDON

PARIS

GO!

I had eaten some food on the train that my stomach couldn't handle and I couldn't sleep all night. I reached home with a blackened face, howling and crying. My mom didn't say 'I told you so' until I got better, but that was my first and last train experience ever. Not counting *Jab We Met*, of course! Trains and I have always been a recipe for disaster, though Geet, my character in the film, made it fun.

I think part of the reason I decided to become an actress was because we get to travel around the world so much. I love the pure thrill of arriving in a new place, and meeting people from different cultures. Also, being famous has a downside: it's next to impossible for me to walk around on the streets in India, or go to my favourite restaurant

to grab a quick bite without being smothered in attention. That's why travelling abroad means freedom to do what I want, whenever I want to.

But vacations and holidays are also the number one reason people slip up on their diet and fitness. And it's all because of the common misconception that being on a diet kills the fun. Well, think again! I am going to show you how you can holiday, have a complete blast and still stick to your diet and fitness regimen. After I signed on to Rujuta's diet plan, my first real test of discipline was the *Tashan* shoot in Ladakh. But she was already ten steps ahead of me. Remember my earlier diet chart—didn't sound too boring, now did it! So instead of hunting for dal-roti-sabzi, I ate traditional momos and thukpa for

Over the years, I've become a seasoned traveller

lunch and dinner. For the *Kambakkht Ishq* shoot in Venice, I feasted on home-made pasta with gorgonzola cheese, along with salad for lunch and dinner. And a little tiramisu, as a reward for being good.

Eating when I'm on holiday is also about the ambience for me. When Saif and I travelled to Gstaad in Switzerland, my favourite travel destination in the world, we would always end up at the fanciest of restaurants. These are the kind of restaurants that serve you the richest, creamiest but most delicious food in the world. One day after a very heavy meal, Saif, ready to pass out from eating, looked at me and said, 'I can't eat this rich fatty food every day. I just want some simple

ghar ka khaana. How in the world are you managing?' I just looked at him in surprise and replied, 'That's coz I'm not eating everything on the menu!' What he didn't realize was that I was going to all these gorgeous eateries to enjoy the ambience and the dining experience. I was happy ordering a salad and soup, which could have been made anywhere, but of course, had the true local flavour and ingredients. But poor Saif was the one who couldn't resist the yummy food and was stuffing himself silly.

Now, whenever I plan a trip, I plan my meals in advance too. Rujuta and I hit the Internet to check out the best restaurants in the area, and make a list of all the things I should eat while I'm

I pack healthy home-made food to eat on the flight, because, let's face it, you can get tired of dried-up airline food pretty fast.

travelling, especially seasonal foods. I also try and pack healthy home-made food to eat on the flight, because, let's face it, you can get tired of dried-up airline food pretty fast. You might not believe me, but I've even made friends with the chef at London Airport, since I pass through that area so many times. He knows exactly how I like my sandwiches, so all I do is call him in advance to let him know what time I'll be dropping by, and there's always a healthy 'Kareena-specific' snack waiting for me. Now that's what I call real service!

And even though vacations are my time to let go, Saif and I try to mix a little exercise into our fun. Except that, in this case, exercise becomes fun, because we can actually step out into the streets or parks without starting a riot. We love going for long walks together in Hyde Park when we're in London, just enjoying the crisp fresh air and greenery. We get a chance to catch up on our chats, and feel just like a normal couple with no one else around. In the mountains, walking uphill for even half an hour will burn more calories than spending two hours in the gym. And if we're off to the Maldives, it's time for some swimming in the crystal clear sea or doing laps in the pool. It never feels like a workout, but it still helps keep the holiday weight off. Not to mention being a great way for couples to keep the romance alive.

THE 15-MINUTE TRAVEL YOGA ROUTINE

I have put this little routine together. It's quick, easy-to-do and a super way to stay in shape while you're holidaying. The best part is you will feel fit and ready for an entire day of fun and indulgence!

KAPALBHATI KRIYA
(25 STROKES, 2 ROUNDS)
• Forcefully exhale through your nose, two strokes in one second. • If you are a beginner, start with 25 strokes (2 rounds) and do it slowly (1 stroke in 1 second). As you get used to it, increase it to 50 strokes (4 rounds). • Advanced practitioners can do 100 strokes (5 rounds) at a stretch.

TRIKONASANA
(10 SECONDS)
• Stand straight with legs together and hands by the side of the thighs. • Slowly move your legs apart at a distance of 2 to 3 feet slowly raising both your hands sideways to shoulder level with the palms facing the floor. • Slowly bend forward towards the right touching the big toe of the right leg with the left hand without bending the knees and raise your right hand up and look up towards the right hand, breathing normally. • Hold this for some time and come back to the starting position. • Repeat on the other side.

PARVATASANA
IN PADMASANA
(HOLD FOR 10 SECONDS)
• Sit straight in padmasana with palms resting on the floor. • Bring your palms together facing each other in namaskar mudra close to the chest. • Slowly inhale and raise your hands upwards and stretch your arms as much as you can without exerting pressure on the neck. • Breathe normally and hold it there for some time and come back to the starting position.

NAUKASANA
(HOLD FOR 10 SECONDS)
• Lie down on your back with your feet together and your palms resting on your thighs. • Inhale and raise both legs up, then raise the upper body off the floor. • Hold it for some time while breathing normally keeping your hands parallel to the floor. • Slowly come back to the starting position.

MAINTAIN YOUR WEIGHT WHILE ON THE GO

BHUJANGASANA
(HOLD FOR 10 SECONDS)
• Lie on your stomach, legs and toes together, toes pointing outward, hands by the side of the body, palms facing upward and forehead on the floor.
• Now bend your hands from the elbows, place the palms on the floor, near each side of the shoulder; your thumb should be under the armpit. • Inhale and raise the chin and turn the head backward as much as possible. • Raise the thorax up to the navel, hold this for some time breathing normally, then while exhaling come down to the starting position.

ANULOM VILOM
(3 ROUNDS)
• Use the thumb of your right hand to close your right nostril and inhale from the left nostril. Then close your left nostril with your right index and middle fingers and exhale from the right nostril. • Now in the reverse manner inhale with the right nostril, close your right nostril with your right thumb then exhale with the left. • This forms one round of anulom--vilom pranayama.

Do It Like I Do!

Your skin and digestion can really take a beating on those long-haul journeys. **Drink more water** to stay well-hydrated on flights.

Take a Vitamin E or flaxseed supplement during the flight. It helps prevent dry chapped lips and skin.

Pack nuts, dried fruits and cheese in your suitcase and hand baggage to snack on. That way, you won't be tempted to satisfy your snack cravings with a packet of chips or choc-chip biscuits.

The most important rule is to **keep breakfast, lunch and dinner local**. Do a little research on the best restaurants around your hotel, and what local dishes match your diet plan. There's no excuse if you have Google on your side.

Always plan for the first meal on arrival: if you eat your first meal right, you will continue eating correctly throughout your trip.

Plan ahead for the dessert or fried foods that you plan to eat. I pick the date and time I'm going to binge on french fries in Bangkok or my favourite cheese fondue in Switzerland. That way, I don't feel I'm indulging myself.

Most hotels have gyms and swimming pools that will help you keep to your exercise regimen. But if they don't, **just walk around.** You'll get to know the place better and burn some calories too.

Travel being my passion, I like to combine it with my other two favourite things: yoga and food. Let's make eating fun now . . . while we take a tour around the world.

EUROPE

Most vegetarians shudder when they think of travelling to this part of the world. They assume they'll be forced to survive on bread, potatoes and water. But I've eaten some of the best meals of my vegetarian life there. In **GREECE**, fava beans served with herb rice is my go-to dish. In **ITALY**, I have gorged on wholegrain pasta with different varieties of cheese and plates piled high with yummy fresh greens. And their minestrone soup is divine. In **FRANCE**, well, you cannot not adore French cuisine.

The country has some of the best farmers' markets in the world. So just ask the waiter for a plate of fresh salads made from the available exotic and fresh vegetables and fruits. Apart from superhot men, **TURKEY** also has skin-friendly hummus, pita bread, bean stews and plenty of fresh greens that you just can't miss. Though, if Saif and I are travelling out of India for more than ten days, we start craving Indian food. It's funny to walk into an Indian restaurant and shock the staff there.

UNITED STATES

Stop thinking burgers, hot dogs, fries and coke. The US offers travellers the widest variety of cuisines from all over the world, and some of the tastiest vegetarian food you'll ever find. Lebanese, Korean, Chinese, North African, French, Thai, and, of course, Indian food is just a short walk down the street. When you're in this part of the world, you need to explore and experiment!

SOUTH-EAST ASIA

It's no secret that my favourite cuisine, apart from ghar ka khaana, is Chinese food. So I make sure to satisfy my craving for noodles, vegetable stir-fry, fried rice and soup whenever I'm travelling east. Try the vegetable Thai curry and steamed rice in Bangkok. It will blow your mind.

Gstaad

I prefer travelling to the mountains, rather than the beach. So, while on holiday, you will usually find me bundled up in warm clothes, sipping wine in front of a fireplace. Saif and I stay at the Gstaad Palace Hotel, where my favourite snack is the avocado sandwich with tomato slices. And the fondue, which has to be literally dragged out of arm's reach or I'll never stop eating. Chesery in Gstaad makes the best home-made breads, my favourite, while Saif loves their grilled meats. And if you're a breakfast person like me, try out the local delicacies and fresh wholegrain breads at Early Beck.

London

I love the mushroom risotto at Gordon Ramsay's at Claridges. And I never leave the city without a meal at Signor Sassi. I also sneak in one stop at China Town for a taste of authentic street food. Wagamama's noodle soup? Heavenly!

New York City

Starbucks! I cannot function without my cup of coffee in the morning and even at home I use Starbucks sachets. So when I'm the in the US, I need to visit a coffee shop at least three times a day. But of course, I keep my promise to Rujuta and bite into a fresh fruit first.

Mumbai

If you're in my city, you have to try my list of recommendations. Elco on Hill Road, my childhood favourite, still has the yummiest paani puri around. My girlfriends and I love gossiping over glasses of wine at Pali Village Cafe in Bandra, and at Olive near Carter Road. Since the Kapoor family is obsessed, fanatic, mad about Chinese food, we satisfy our cravings by planning a meal at China House at the Grand Hyatt or Royal China in Bandra.

New Delhi

Spice Route at the Imperial Hotel makes a wide variety of authentic Thai food that I crave whenever I'm in the capital. Le Cirque at The Leela also makes some of the best French food in India.

THE ROLE-PLAYING GODDESS

My family keeps teasing me saying that I was born a star. Or at least that's what I behaved like from day one. There was no denying that I was every bit a drama queen with a flair for theatrics! Even though we had a very regular childhood—homework, crushes and heartbreak—the Kapoor acting gene was always in my blood, and I lived and breathed movies.

For a short time I was convinced I wanted to be a lawyer. I don't know what I was thinking. Maybe I had seen a movie with a hotshot lawyer as the star and thought I'd be better in that role. But thank God that phase was very short-lived. I would have lost

every case because I'm always late, so I'd have never made it to the court on time. Lolo started acting when she was just sixteen, and, as you already know, I was dazzled by her life. I was forever excited to be around the costumes, watch the dances being choreographed and see my favourite actors right in front of my eyes. But apart from getting me wide-eyed with wonder, this also gave me a chance to be on set at a pretty young age. At that time, if you had told Salman Khan or Aamir Khan that they would one day be romancing me on screen, they would have probably punched you in the face. I was Lolo's baby sister, so by default, I became everybody's chhoti behen.

I remember being on the sets of *Raja Hindustani*, the film which made Lolo a huge star. I would hang out with Manish Malhotra, who was the costume designer at that time, and he would let me look at the clothes and sometimes even take me shopping with him. Things were very different then: no stylists, no lookbooks, no hair-and-make-up meetings. The director would just say, 'The scene is set in Switzerland' and the costume designer would come up with five chiffon saris in different colours for the heroine to choose from. Never mind that she'd be freezing and no woman in her right mind would ever wear a chiffon sari on top of a mountain. But that's the magic of Indian movies!

One of the highlights for me at that time was this one particular trip to the UK with my sister and Mom. The film got shelved, but Manish and I had tons of fun travelling around Liverpool, Manchester and Blackpool. We bought clothes and stuffed ourselves with the yummiest junk food we could find.

When I finally decided to take the plunge and make my film debut in 2000, I was already absolutely comfortable on a movie set. I had unknowingly seen the business from inside out. Of course, the media picked up on the fact that I was soon going to make my Bollywood debut.

But my biggest high isn't tracking box-office figures or seeing my face in the papers. It's having my fans connect with me.

And they did the obvious: compared me with my sister and stressed on my Kapoor legacy. There was a lot riding on whether I would make it or not. The pressure was on! But kudos to my parents for raising me to become a confident and determined woman because of which I never felt like there was a sword hanging above my head. I was doing what I always wanted to do, and that made me the happiest girl in the world.

Soon *Refugee* hit the big screen and the rest as they say is history! I've always done things my way and I went on to act my heart out on 70 mm. It's been a rollercoaster ride. I'm blessed that I've had more hits than misses, and today they call me the 'Rs 100 crore heroine'. But my biggest high isn't tracking box-office figures or seeing my face in the papers. It's having my fans connect with me, support me and shower me with their love and blessings. It is strange how much fashion and style have become a part of my journey as a leading actress in India. When I look back now, my films form a sort of storyboard with each character taking a life of her own. Some have even become iconic now. Hearing that the chikan kurti/patiala pants combination I'm wearing in a film is being copied by every college girl from Mumbai to Mohali, that's when I know I'm exactly where I was meant to be.

HIGH STREET

Kabhi Kushi Kabhie Gham

Red bustier top, shiny red pants and *You are my Soniya*. That was the look that started it all. Hrithik and I were back on screen as a romantic couple, which obviously made everybody sit up and take notice. My character, Pooja Sharma, better known as Poo, was this happy-go-lucky, clueless-about-life but-very-clued-into-fashion uber cool girl. Karan Johar and Manish had really gone over every single detail to make my clothes truly trendy. Each character had a specially designed wardrobe to match their personality. Poo, of course, was high-street-meets-designer-wear! It was also the first time an actress was wearing expensive designer clothes from Dolce & Gabbana to Versace in a Hindi movie. My red outfit in the song was quite a fluke though. I remember the leather pants were a bit difficult to dance in, so Manish decided to cut the bottoms and make slits. And that became a huge rage and a fashion trend! My stomach was exposed in that song, which I was actually quite happy about because I had worked quite a bit to get into shape for that. The entire film was very well-styled, but this particular look got such a huge reaction that even I was surprised. It easily became one of the most stylish and recognizable characters ever to feature on the big screen. I guess it also started the trend of red being my lucky colour on screen. To top it all, I was nominated for a *Filmfare* award for Best Supporting Actress. Talk about living the dream!

THE HIGH-STREET CHICK LOOK

Poo's look was all about being young, bold and modern. Lucky for you, everyone's wearing colourful pants right now, so finding a pair of red bottoms isn't going to be hard. Opt for a colour-blocked look by pairing it with hot pink, fuchsia or bright coral for a unique take on the *You are my Soniya* style. But go easy on the make-up, or you'll look like a traffic signal. Just a nude lipstick and tons of mascara is all you need. And don't forget that hipster attitude!

Asoka

When I first signed on this movie, I couldn't have been more excited. It was a dream to be acting opposite Shah Rukh Khan and be directed by Santosh Sivan. Santosh wanted me to do something that Indian actresses very rarely pull off right: appear on screen without much make-up and ooze oomph. It was a very risky move, and many people told me I was crazy to try it. But that was exactly what attracted me to the character: the chance to do away with all the frills and fusses of being a star and let my talent speak for itself. It helped that my character Princess Kaurwaki was strong, beautiful and independent, the three traits that I really respect in a person. The look was so striking that every single review mentioned the styling of my character. I loved the simplicity of the dramatic eyes and bare face, which was actually the base of the whole look. Even the costumes were very minimalist, mostly midriff-baring old-world saris. The saris were very technical, because they had to be draped in such a way that they didn't add bulk to my body. They also crimped my hair to give it that wild, warrior-princess feel. Drama, drama and more drama.

THE WARRIOR-PRINCESS LOOK

A Grecian one-shouldered toga dress in eggshell or a cream cotton sari with a gold border will work as a fantastic base for this look. The hair shouldn't be perfectly blow-dried; instead, let it air-dry after adding a little styling mousse so that you get those gorgeous natural waves. Your lips need to be completely bare, so smear on that moisturizing chapstick and nothing else. Princess Kaurwaki's intensity was all in the eyes. So your eyes need proper highlighting: go for the smoky-eye look or use a thick liner and kajal and tons of mascara. Try drawing out the eyeliner to give the 1960s cat's eye effect for added drama. Jewellery should be earthy, so try loads of chunky wooden and enamel bangles, but leave the neck and ears bare.

Chameli

Playing a prostitute won me my first *Filmfare* Best Actress award. That only proved my point: that making bold choices and following your heart will earn you success. I have to thank Sudhir Mishra for making a film that had a lead heroine instead of a hero, and for believing that I could be that girl. When I told my friends that I would be playing a prostitute, I think most of them didn't know how to react. I was told that it would damage my career to play a character with such negative shades so early on. But thank God I was too brash and stubborn to listen to anyone's advice. One of the biggest struggles of the film was to find a costume that wouldn't seem dull on screen, because Chameli wears just one outfit throughout the movie. Manish was absolutely adamant that we use vibrant colours to make her stand out against the darker background of the film. We did a photo shoot with a few options for the costume. Everybody unanimously fell in love with the red sari and that was the look they finally locked. My colourful blouse with three-quarter sleeves was bought from Khar market in Mumbai, and since the sari couldn't look expensive, the stylists bought six identical pieces of artificial georgette. The hair was given thick waves, and I wore a flower clip on one side, an ode to the flower my character was named after. They decided to give me red lipstick to match the sari and make the whole look pop even more. I was a bit sceptical about the plunging neckline, but it was integral to the character who was supposed to be seducing men for a living. That look is still one of my favourites, because it's etched into everybody's mind so clearly. The whole package was perfect: a great script, a tough role and a film that was centred completely around me.

THE BOLD-SEDUCTRESS LOOK

Though Chameli was a streetwalker, she never looked slutty or cheap. And that's the beauty of this look. If you're unsure of copying her plunging neckline, how about switching it for an interesting design on the back of a printed choli with three-quarter sleeves? That way, you can be sexy without being too in-your-face. Pair that with a sari in a solid colour, with a bright lip to match. The focus should primarily be on the lips, while keeping everything else very muted. There's a shade of red out there for every woman, so once you have found the perfect one for your skin tone, use it with confidence.

Kambakkht Ishq

This movie may not have set the box office on fire, but it will never be forgotten for the super-glamorous clothes and sky-high heels. I was in London and my stylist, Aki Narula, had gone to Milan to shop for the wardrobe. When he was done, I actually flew home to Mumbai for just six hours, to try on the entire loot—sixty-three outfits in all, not to mention forty-seven pairs of shoes with the highest heels I had ever attempted to wear in my life. My mom was sitting in the bedroom watching the mini fashion show, and the big smile on her face made it clear that she was loving everything. She even told Aki that she'd never seen me look more beautiful! This is a massive compliment coming from someone with very discerning taste. Once the promos hit the air, even my friends couldn't get enough of the looks. It was probably the first time the concept of colour-blocking was used in such a bold manner, since we were pairing electric-purple dresses with blood-red shoes and parrot-green clutches. It was like living in Barbie's world, and for a woman who loves to play with fashion, it was like I had died and gone to wardrobe heaven. For the courtroom scene, I was wearing a really complicated ruffled dress, and a Mohawk bun in my hair. So many of my friends were dying to know where the dress was from, because they wanted to get similar ones. After the movie released, I could see a visible effect even on the way people dressed in the streets. Suddenly, we were embracing colour again, instead of everybody opting for the safe Little Black Dress, and people weren't afraid to let their individuality show.

THE SUPERMODEL LOOK

The *Kambakkht Ishq* girl is unabashedly sexy. She has the body of a supermodel, and she's not afraid to show it off in micro miniskirts and fitted dresses. She also knows which colours work for her skin tone, and is not afraid to experiment with multiple colours in a single outfit. The hair is also really slick and set in place, rather than being bohemian and free-flowing, teamed with killer make-up. And don't forget the heels. As high as you can manage without toppling over and definitely in a colour that contrasts with your dress.

Tashan

The size-zero phenomenon. That is how *Tashan* will always be remembered, thanks to the media frenzy over my new size. More than the looks in the movie, I think people were looking at my body with a magnifying glass and trying to figure out how a chubby Punjabi girl had morphed into a super-toned diva. It was the green bikini scene that stole the show, though. Nobody thought they'd ever see a Kapoor girl in a two-piece on screen; neither did I for that matter. But I trusted Yash Raj and when Adi Chopra said I needed to wear a bikini, I didn't argue. I was always a confident girl, never too worried about how I looked, but this was new for me too. I couldn't wait to see the reactions, dying to know if all my hard work had paid off. The film released, and my phone went mad. People were calling and messaging me non-stop for days. Everyone wanted to know one thing. 'Oh my God, how did you do it?' And now you know! That phase was one of the biggest highs of my life. I have to admit I love looking at the photos from that movie, just to see how toned and well-defined my body was. *Tashan* wasn't about a statement wardrobe, it was about making a statement: 'There's nothing Kareena Kapoor can't do.'

THE TONED-BODY LOOK

Apart from the bikini, the one look that really had people talking was the knotted white shirt and hot shorts combo. Start with a pair of denim shorts, which, if you don't already have one, you should step out right this minute and buy. The look is really about showing off a toned body, so don't be afraid to go as short as you can without feeling uncomfortable. Get one with shredded hems or rips in it to give it a bit of character. Next, get out your boyfriend's white shirt, one that's just a little too big for you. Leave the last three buttons undone and knot it up. You could show off just a tiny peek of your midriff, provided you have the abs to pull it off, of course. Aviator sunglasses and a little bronzer on your cheekbones and jawline, and you'll have jaws dropping everywhere you go.

Jab We Met

For the narration of *Jab We Met*, I was sitting with the director Imtiaz Ali, Shahid Kapoor and Manish. When we took a break, Manish looked at me and said, 'This is your movie.' And I couldn't agree more. *Jab We Met* was a career-defining film for me. Suddenly, people were seeing me in a completely new avatar. And let me tell you, being casual on screen is the most difficult thing to do. Intense scenes are easy. The more drama it requires, the easier the actor's job becomes. It's trying to put energy into something like a simple conversation without being melodramatic which is really the acid test. To be excited and bubbly without going over the top was the challenge. And I pulled it off! But what I did not expect was Geet becoming a trendsetter! The T-shirt and salwar combination happened by chance. It was supposed to be a night scene and Imtiaz, who has such a fantastic eye for detail, was trying to figure out what I would wear to bed on a train. Since I was already wearing a salwar kurta, they decided that my character would change the top and put on a T-shirt, something as natural and simple as that. Nobody knew that would become the talking point of the film. Next thing I know, young girls everywhere were wearing the same combination to college. Street stores around India were flooded with printed salwars, harem pants and casual tees, because suddenly it had become the hottest selling item, and the look is copied even today. It's the only film where the childishness and innocence with which this happy-go-lucky girl wore her clothes became a style statement. Even Shobhaa Dé called *Jab We Met* the 'most styled film' of that year. For the last song, Manish decided to glam up the salwar-top combo by designing a black corset with harem pants. Geet became so iconic that even Madame Tussauds decided that she was the one they wanted as the concept for my wax statue. And who am I to argue with that?

THE GIRL-NEXT-DOOR LOOK

Geet was spontaneous and fun-loving, and that's exactly what your wardrobe should reflect if this is your kind of style. Think printed or slogan tees paired with loose-fitting harem or patiala pants in a solid colour. You could also pair a chikan kurta in your favourite colour with a pair of dark-wash skinny jeans for a versatile look that can take you from office/college to dinner with friends. Don't overload on jewellery: just a simple pair of silver earrings paired with some colourful bangles are all you need. Along with the unbeatable I-love-myself-best attitude to carry off this look!

3 Idiots

This is one of my favourite films, not just because it had Aamir Khan and Raju Hirani, but because I was allowed to roam around in jeans and T-shirts all day. Just kidding! The funny part is even though the look was so simple and casual, tons of detailing went into creating my character Pia's wardrobe. We had hundreds of fittings, even though I was in track pants and T-shirts for most of the scenes. Raju had a very clear idea of what he wanted me to look like, and the glasses were his suggestion. Working with him has taught me how important styling is for the audience to accept a character. It was a new look for me, but I fell in love with it instantly. Then for the *Zoobie Doobie* song, Manish picked out that gorgeous dress with tons of volume so that Aamir and I would really look like we were floating away on clouds. I used to twirl around in my trailer in that dress, dancing in front of the mirror. It felt just like something from a fairy tale.

THE GEEKY-GLAM LOOK

This look was really defined by the glasses. There's something about glasses that makes a woman look intensely serious and wonderfully awkward at the same time. The look is so popular today that I see a lot of people wearing statement glasses even if they're not numbered. The bigger the better. You can even get them in different colours to have a little more fun. For the hair, a side braid is the way to go. Slightly messy, but still more interesting than a plain braid or ponytail, the side plait is one of the hottest hairstyles at the moment.

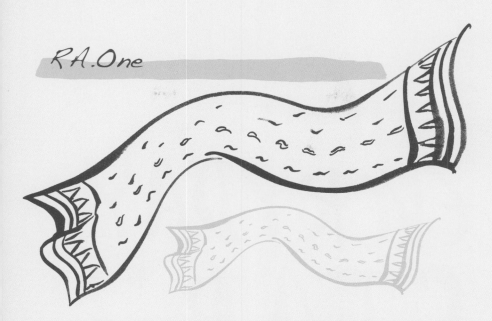

R.A.One

At a time when songs decide the fate of a movie, I think *Chammak Challo* became the biggest hit of that year. And my red sari, like every other time I've picked that colour to wear in a movie, was a super-duper hit. It was actually made as a full sari for the train sequence, but when I had to dance in it, I asked for something a little lighter. And actually, it was Ganesh Acharya and Shah Rukh Khan who decided to take off the pallu and wrap it around my waist like a sarong. Manish had to pre-stitch the pallu so that it wouldn't fall off, and he decided to cheat with the blouse. Nobody noticed, but the sari blouse was changed for one with net sleeves in the song. He also insisted I wear a nose-ring to add a little sexiness to the character. My curves were back and it really paid off. Karan called to congratulate me, saying, 'Darling, you're looking super hot.' Even Saif couldn't take his eyes off the screen when he first saw the dance. I think he took me out to dinner and pampered me a little extra that night. If you ask me, I think my body has never looked better than in that song.

THE CHAMMAK-CHALLO LOOK

Since red is something of a sure-hit success formula for me, the sari you pick for this look has to be red too. Play with the length of the sleeves using transparent net, and you can even have interesting embellishments added on to them. The nose ring is an inseparable part of the look, and the good news is you don't have to have a piercing to wear one. Just a little clip-on will do the trick. And don't forget to celebrate your curves!

THE EVERYDAY STAR!

What do you think a movie star wears when she's at home? Diamond necklaces and Louis Vuitton dressing gowns? Actually, it's a Fab India printed cotton kaftan. Shapeless and soft with a zipper in front. A little granny-auntyish, but I just love how comfortable they are. I have three favourite ones that get softer every time they're washed. Hmm . . . perfectly snuggle-worthy. So if you ever drop in on me at home unannounced, that's probably what I'll be wearing when I open the door.

The problem is if I have a favourite garment, I tend to live in it. Whenever I get a day off from shooting, all I do is lie around the house in my kaftan the whole day, catching up on my favourite TV shows and girlie gossip with my friends. Trying to get me to change into anything more respectable won't work. Trust me, they've all tried. My mom makes fun of me the most. She keeps saying, 'How can you wear those ugly things? I used to wear them when I was pregnant with you.' Saif hates them too; he keeps plotting to burn them or throw them out. But I've

dressing according to the weather. I'm not one of those silly women who'll sweat to death in a pair of boots just because someone says that's what's trendy right now.

That's really my simplest rule to getting fashion right. Weather! What's the point in getting carried away and buying Burberry trench coats and knee-high boots when you live on the west coast of India and winter means it's 25 degrees outside. It's fine if you're living in England, or when you travel often to colder climates, but otherwise it's just a waste of money.

My second big rule is comfort. If you don't know anything else about my style, you should know this: I refuse to wear clothes that are itchy, scratchy, stiff, tight, too short, too heavy, rough, suffocating or ugly. I guess that explains my obsession with kaftans. It doesn't matter how gorgeous the dress or how expensive—if it's frilly and fussy and needs to be adjusted constantly, I'm never going to wear it. Even the most stunning dress could ruin your evening if you have to constantly adjust the neckline, or make sure the hemline doesn't ride up.

Once I leave the house, I should forget what I'm wearing and just be free. Maybe I'll just turn up to a party in my kaftan one day and see if it starts a trend . . . you'll thank me for that later. But until then, my absolute favourite piece of clothing has to be that perfect pair of jeans!

made it clear how much I love them. So he's made his peace!

If I have to head out of the house, and it's not a cocktail party or red carpet affair, this is what I'm most likely to look like: wearing blue jeans and white T-shirt, hair pulled into a ponytail and no make-up. Not very exciting, I know. But that's the truth. I've always been a jeans-and-T-shirt girl. As a teenager that was almost my uniform, dressed up or down depending on the occasion. Living in a hot and humid city like Mumbai, I strongly believe in

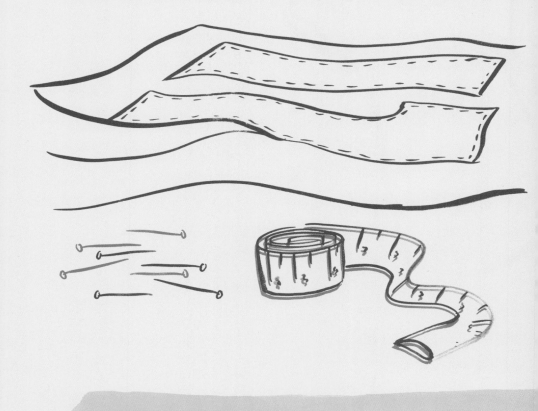

I bought my first pair of 501s when I was ten years old, and they had me at boot-cut. I must have worn that till the buttons fell off. Even now, Saif jokes that my closet looks like the storage facility at Levi's, packed with about forty pairs at last count. In my defence, the reason there are so many is because I've kept a few of the 24-inch, size-zero versions I bought at that time, which I'm holding on to just in case . . .

A good pair of jeans is like the perfect boyfriend: sturdy, low-maintenance and only gets better with time. It's also my back-up plan for any occasion. Running late for a script-reading? Just pull on a straight leg Paige classic pair, find a clean beige V-neck and rush out the door. Cocktail party and the zip of my Roberto Cavalli strapless dress is stuck? 7 For All Mankind boot-cut jeans with a super-high heel and a shimmery top come to my rescue, and no one will ever know the difference.

And the best part? You don't have

According to me, you can't really call anything jeans unless they're blue.

to pay a bomb to look like one. When I was recently shopping in London (my favourite fashion destination in the world!), I discovered a whole world of lesser-known brands at Selfridges. Brand after brand offering fantastic fits without ridiculous price tags. Looking at all those options, from dark wash and clean fades to bright colours and rips—it was amazing to see how far we've come from the '80s stonewash, which, let's be honest, didn't flatter anyone. Though, according to me, you can't really call anything jeans unless they're blue. All the red, green and mustard versions that everybody's wearing now we should call pants or trousers, or invent a new term for them. Anything except jeans.

Another trick I've learnt to make the best use of my denims is not to wash them too much. Jeans are meant to be used and abused. I'm the kind of girl who doesn't wash hers in a month. In fact, I sleep better on a flight in a pair that's really worn in.

Denim Shopping Checklist

 Before you even start shopping, pull out the entire pile in your wardrobe for a test run. If your older pairs exhibit any of these symptoms, get rid of them now!

- I follow a simple five-year-rule. If I haven't worn it in five years, chances are I'm not going to miss it!
- If you've put on a bit of weight, your skinny jeans probably make you look like a walking German sausage.
- Some pairs tend to start bagging around the knee and crotch areas earlier than you might have expected. Don't bother holding on to them to justify the price tag; just put it down to bad luck and go shopping for a sturdier pair.

 Giving those forgotten pairs away helps make space for more. I call that good shopping karma.

 Take account of what you have and what you don't. The basic pairs you should have in your wardrobe at any given point of time include your good ol' faithful casual regular fit, your top-of-the-line dressy pair that will look as good on a runway as a couture gown and the one you can tug on for a movie or a casual night out. These three are staples; the rest you can have as much fun with as possible!

 If you haven't bought a pair in months, it might be a good idea to find a measuring tape and jot down your vital stats. We've all had those moments when we've carried an armful of 28-inch-waist jeans into the dressing room, only to find out we should have gone with 30. There's no point learning the truth in the trial room.

 A huge shopping tip I've never forgotten is to always try on a pair before buying it. Even if you've been buying from the same brand for years, each pair of jeans is cut differently. A three-way mirror in the dressing room will make sure you won't be disappointed when you get home.

 I can't say this enough but like most women, I prefer shopping to be a group sport. I've been talked out of making some big mistakes, thanks to a friend's honest critique. Taking Amrita or my sister along has saved me from making some bad buys in the past. Shopping companions can hold your place in the queue at the trial room while you hunt for a different size or help find a good option you didn't spot yourself.

Settle on a Style

BOOT-CUT

I'm a boot-cut girl. A little flare at the bottom gives the bum a good shape, and balances out the typical Indian hourglass figure. I like to separate my jeans into casual day pairs and slightly classier night options. A classic dark blue boot-cut paired with peep-toe pumps makes me feel as sexy as if I was wearing those short dresses that everybody's running around in.

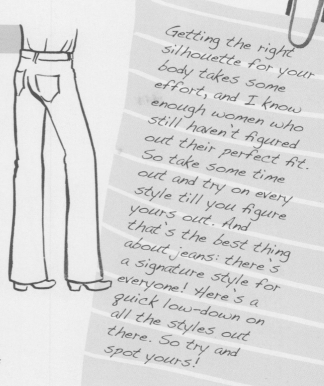

Getting the right silhouette for your body takes some effort, and I know enough women who still haven't figured out their perfect fit. So take some time out and try on every style till you figure yours out. And that's the best thing about jeans: there's a signature style for everyone! Here's a quick low-down on all the styles out there. So try and spot yours!

The golden rules of denim buying

1 It's fitted at the waistline and hips, without cutting into your stomach.
2 The hem reaches down an inch past your ankle. This makes the pair versatile enough to be worn with flats and heels without trailing on the floor. Else, get it cut and hemmed at the store itself! 3 It's got enough stretch in the fabric to allow you to dance, bend or sit cross-legged effortlessly. Do a little jig with it in the trial room if you have to be sure. 4 The waistline is high enough to protect your assets when you bend or sit down. The trend of having your panties flash over the top of your jeans never really took off. So let's just forget that dark phase in fashion history. 5 And finally the most important: make sure your butt looks good. Else you're throwing money down the drain.

JEANS

SKINNY
Despite what every woman wants to believe, skinny jeans only really work for those with long slim legs. So, if you're lady-long-legs, you know what to pick! And if you're wearing boots over your jeans, stick to skinny. Nothing's worse than crumpled denim bulging out of your slick boots. If you've got thick calves like me, you can get away with tucking them into boots.

STRAIGHT CUT
Instead of wishing you looked like Kate Moss, trick your body into feeling long and lean with jeans that are cut straight on the leg. They skim past the calves, hug the thighs, and give the illusion of supermodel stems. This is one of the best denim innovations when it comes to camouflage!

BOYFRIEND
This only works on slim tall women. Yes, it's unfair, but would you rather look like someone drowned you in the laundry bag? A clever way to work around the trend is to buy a shredded pair with a straight leg, and fold up the hemline. It's a healthy compromise.

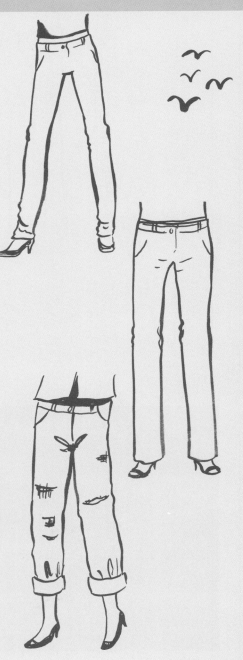

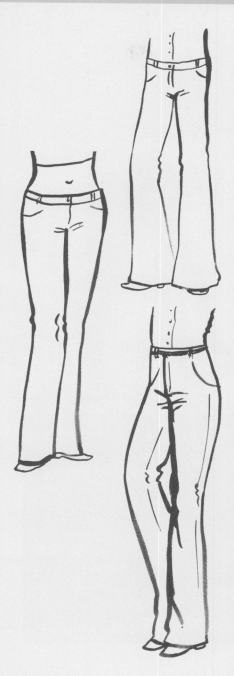

FLARE

When it's in vogue, it's a rage and when not, it can be a complete fashion faux pas. The flare can be as dramatic as bell bottoms or a more conservative A-line; either way, check your fashion report before you try this one on!

LOW RISE

This is a tricky one! If you're super toned, show off that mean waist and hips. But if you're even slightly flabby, stay far away from this style as it tends to dig into your stomach and hips and create that dreaded muffin top. When you're trying these out bend over, crouch and sit to ensure you don't show off your behind!

HIGH WAIST

I like the whole retro vibe of the high-waist jeans that some brands offer. But those only suit women with tiny waists and proportionate hips because they emphasize your figure, rather than camouflage it. And if you're pear-shaped, be ready for some very honest answers to the 'Does this make me look fat?' question.

JEANS

Favourite Brands

You can't go wrong with Levi's. They're cheap and comfortable, and have so many options to choose from that you really don't have to try too hard to find a good pair. Not to mention it's tradition to own one.

Paige is my new favourite, though it's not available in India. Simple classic styles are the most versatile.

Another not-too-expensive brand that I discovered in London is Marrakech which makes lovely silhouettes for curvy women.

7 For All Mankind are a bit more formal, perfect for a party when you're not in the mood to wear a dress.

I also love J Brand and Citizens of Humanity for making jeans that respect the curves of real women and give them the best shape.

You can't go wrong with Levi's. They're cheap and comfortable.

Denim Faux Pas!

1 Paint splatters. I cannot repeat this enough. It doesn't matter if your favourite actress was spotted wearing them to a Page 3 party, looking like a lost construction worker was never fashionable. And while we're on the subject, no cloth patches either. Why would you want to look like trash on purpose? **2** Sequins and embroidery on jeans were popular when I was a teenager. They haven't been since. **3** While I think torn jeans and a white shirt is the perfect look, it could go horribly wrong. The key is to find a pair with well-placed rips, ideally near the knee or lower thigh. Any higher than that and you might be giving your audience more than they paid for.

TOPS

T-shirts

Buying T-shirts is guilt-free shopping. In fact, if I had a choice between buying expensive jewellery or a simple T-shirt, I'd go with the second option. Black, white and grey tees go with anything. You can wear your jeans for ages without washing them, but tops tend to lose their shape quickly, so I never feel bad about tossing them out and making room for new ones. Or if I can't bear to part with a particular favourite, I just turn it into my night shirt, even if it has holes in it.

My personal style is pretty Los Angeles street, so I've taken a liking to wearing loose tops with leggings. This is also the usual trend spotted on Hollywood celebrities on Rodeo Drive. It's so much cooler to give an interview in something comfortable and trendy rather than in tight dresses that just look like you're trying too hard. In movies like *Golmaal 2* and *3 Idiots* my characters were dressed in colourful T-shirts with cargo pants or jeans the whole time. Coz the look spells casual like nothing else! The slogan T-shirts from *Golmaal* became a huge hit with college girls, and I got many letters thanking me for making funny, quirky T-shirts cool again. I guess my personal style tends to influence my movie looks too, and this is a look I wear all the time off screen.

Sometimes, I'll even steal Saif's tees and wear them out on a pair of jeans. His tight T-shirts often look better on me, though he's never going to admit that. Since men don't have too many options for outerwear, I have a sneaky suspicion designers compensate by making their clothes softer. Even if we buy from the same brand, somehow, his shirts always feel better on the body than mine. So, you can't blame me for being a T-shirt thief. Besides, that just gives me an excuse to buy him even more comfy clothes, so nobody can complain.

Cropped or short tees keep returning as fashion trends, but you really should avoid them unless you have washboard abs.

It's All about the Length!

The style I prefer the most is T-shirts that are slightly loose or A-line and end two inches below the stomach. That's the most versatile look, and works well when paired with jeans, trousers and skirts. It also suits almost every body type, so you don't have to worry about tummy tyres or back fat bulging through. Though, if you are wearing something body-hugging, make sure the fabric isn't too thin or every little spot of cellulite will be exposed.

Cropped or short tees keep returning as fashion trends, but you really should avoid them unless you have washboard abs. Besides, I wouldn't recommend going out on the streets in India wearing T-shirts that expose your navel.

T-shirt dresses should be worn with jeggings or leggings. Make sure the T-shirt covers your crotch at the front, and hits halfway on your butt at the back. Anything shorter just seems vulgar. I love Topshop tights in basic colours, and they look fantastic when paired with my favourite long tees.

Shirts

Whether you're a man or a woman, do yourself a favour and buy a tailored white shirt. The brands that I swear by are Ann Fontaine, Dolce & Gabbana, Prada, Ralph Lauren and, for a budget buy, Zara. There's nothing sexier than a crisp white shirt and jeans, and it's such a versatile look that you can wear it to work or a party and still make heads turn. Take your time when buying the right shirt, because different styles suit different body types. Colour options are endless with shirts, so suit yourself and the mood.

- If you're top-heavy, stay away from anything that has frills or ruffles on the chest. That will only accentuate your bust and make you look like a giant wedding cake. Also, deep necks work better than high necks to camouflage this area.
- If you have chubby arms, Victorian-style peasant sleeves will hide the flab while adding a feminine touch. I love the simple new silken shirts that just flow over the body rather than cling to it. It's Parisian luxe, weather-friendly, and you can pair it with a pencil skirt/fitted black tuxedo trousers and stilettos for an evening out. Très chic.
- For straight-shaped bodies, tailored shirts in a nice thick fabric can also give the illusion of a slim waist, even if you're still working on getting one. Adding a thick belt might help take off some inches, though you shouldn't overdo it to the point where you can't breathe. If you already have a lovely waistline, wear a thin belt over your shirt to accentuate it.

Vests

This is the single most versatile piece of clothing in my cupboard. I buy them wherever I spot a good fit in a nice stretchy fabric, because you can really never have enough, especially in Mumbai weather. Even if you're not a shopaholic like me, you should have at least four pairs, white, black, grey and nude/beige, which can then be layered under jackets or shirts, or even worn as they are for a sporty, summery look. Try them on with a pair of ripped jeans. That's a pretty, sexy party look, when worn with a pair of killer heels.

I like a simple scooped neck for day wear, and a strong racer-back tee for working out. If you're going out to a dinner party, you could just throw a short cropped jacket over the ganji, add a statement necklace, and that's good enough. Oh, don't forget your bottoms, of course!

The best thing about the ganji is that you don't need to buy them from expensive brands or designer stores. High-street shops usually stock them in a variety of colours, and I've even found a really durable grey tank top on a random shopping street in Bangkok, which has lasted almost three years. They're also small enough to roll up and stuff into the corner of your suitcase, so they're a smart option for emergency extras on long trips.

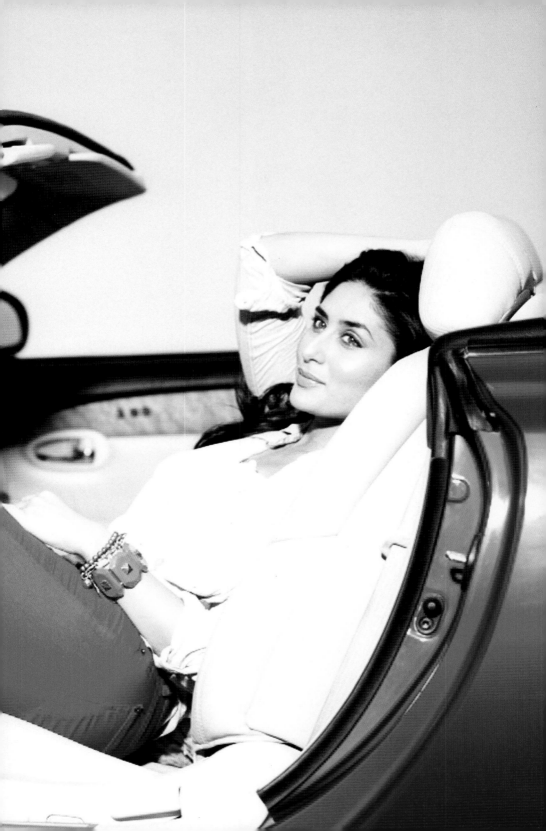

Jackets and Sweaters

India is versatile when it comes to weather. So depending on where you live you'll need more or less of your winter wardrobe. Also even if you're in a perpetually warm city like Mumbai, unless you're extremely boring and like staying in one place, chances are you'll do a bit of travelling to where the temperature is cooler. Here are a couple of essentials you must have:

Imagine you have to go out on a movie date, where it can get a little chilly. Would you rather drag along a granny shawl or layer up in a sexy knit cardi? So get that coquettish cardi and pick a colour that suits your skin tone!

An argyle print sweater, or one with funky motifs can really add sass to your wardrobe. And spruce up the boring old navy and black sweaters, which become a sort of winter uniform!

Waistcoats keep drifting in and out of the hot-trend list, but they're a fun way to go androgynous without looking like a man. Short ones in bright pop colours are great for a casual look, and can be layered over a contrasting tee.

Every woman past the age of twenty should have at least one classy dinner jacket in her cupboard. You never know when the situation demands that you be formally dressed, and a jacket is an instant-glam accessory. Think rich colour, something that reaches down an inch past the top of your jeans, and is fitted at the waist. If you're one of those talented women who really know how to mix and match, buy one in a funky colour. The faint-hearted can opt for a basic colour with a funky printed lining, which only reveals itself in flashes. That's one way to keep them guessing.

A basic trench and an overcoat. The styles are endless, so pick one that suits your frame. Try a neutral colour if you don't want to overload your winter wardrobe. But if you're daring enough, pick a jewelled toned one for a nice bold dash of colour!

Printed vs Plain

I think you've guessed by now that I'm not a fan of big prints. They can be fun sometimes, and I like some of the pretty floral prints you see on shirts, which look so feminine and pretty. But I think you can go horribly wrong if you don't pick the right design for your body and personality. Big prints can overwhelm a petite frame, or draw attention to a larger body shape. Polka dots are fun and retro, but that really depends on the size of the dots and the colour combination. If it's too loud, you just might land up hypnotizing everyone around you, or giving them a bad headache. Vintage prints are kind of cool, though again,

they have to match your personality. Everyone knows I'm not a heavy metal fan, so wearing a ripped Metallica T-shirt will just make me look fake and wannabe. Multi-coloured stripes are really popular on T-shirts, and can really dress up a simple outfit. But remember the golden rule: curvy girls should go vertical, skinny girls can do horizontal.

And finally, no giant studs, patches or rhinestones, please. It just looks so tacky and cheap, even if you've actually gone to a branded store and spent a bomb on it. The cleaner the surface of your top, the less likely you are to be fined by the fashion police.

Favourite Brands

- The best T-shirts for my shape (tall and curvy) are made by Dolce & Gabbana and Wild Fox.
- My favourite brand for basic shirts is Thomas Pink: they cut their clothes like a dream.
- Alexander McQueen is my go-to-designer for loose flowing tops, my new addiction.
- Topshop, Zara and Superdry are my top high-street labels for their variety of T-shirt options.

DRESSES

I just love how wearing a floaty chiffon dress makes me feel like I'm walking on clouds.

Dresses

As much as I say I'm a jeans-and-T-shirt girl, and I really mean it, I do appreciate what a beautiful dress can do for a woman. It's the ultimate definition of feminine glamour, and wearing one instantly changes the way you carry yourself. Usually for the better. Designers like Roberto Cavalli, Roland Mouret and MaxMara are sheer geniuses in the dress department. I'm in a 'maxi' phase right now, and I just love how wearing a floaty chiffon dress makes me feel like I'm walking on clouds.

The first time I tried one for a public event was when I was promoting *Ek Main Aur Ekk Tu*. Rhea Kapoor and Tania Ghavri, who is now my stylist, brought over a bunch of options for me to choose from.

I saw a beige Vanessa Bruno floral dress in the pile, and the moment I tried it on, I knew that was it. Of course it was all over the Internet the next day, but everybody had nothing but nice things to say. Now, even when I'm shopping on my own, I find myself naturally moving towards the maxi-dresses section. Add a thigh high slit and a pair of heels . . . perfection!

I've realized that men love to see their women in dresses, and Saif is always the first one to comment if I'm wearing one in his favourite colour. Even when Tania comes over to the house with her loot, I like trying them on and showing him, just to see his reaction. If his eyes light up and he starts smiling like a little boy in a toy store, the dress stays.

The Must-Haves

THE LBD

The Little Black Dress is an institution, and looks good on women of all ages, sizes and skin tones. It's also the easiest thing to dress up. You don't have to bother about finding a matching pair of shoes or a bag; anything goes. It's also the most versatile option in your wardrobe and can be worn to a cocktail party, dinner, meeting or funeral—just by changing your accessories. I love the classic styles of Ralph Lauren. For a little extra get yourself a LWD, a little white dress. It's fun and flirty and completely in tune with the Indian weather!

THE WRAP

The wrap dress is the perfect silhouette for any body shape. It fits mine to a T, cinching the waist and floating over my Kapoor hips and thighs without accentuating them. The V neckline also supports the bust without revealing too much skin. Though Diane Von Furstenberg is the original brain behind this magical design, you will find many imitations on the high street, so there's a wrap dress out there for every budget. If you're worried about looking too much like your mom, add some sex appeal by wearing a halter-neck version, or even just a sleeveless one with a plunging neckline. I wore a simple black Just Cavalli wrap to the *RA. One wrap-up party* (I thought I'd go with the theme) and though it took me about 15 minutes to get dressed, it looked perfectly pulled together.

The Must-Haves

THE MAXI

When worn right, it can lengthen the body and make you seem taller than you really are. Trust me, it's one of my favourite red-carpet tricks. Since I can't wear my kaftan out on the streets this is as close as it gets to being really comfortable. You don't have to worry about a strong wind lifting your skirt Marilyn-Monroe style, and since the length covers your entire leg, you can even get away without making a trip to the beauty parlour. And ladies, we know how much of a blessing that can be. Since the maxi already has so much fabric, you really have to play a balancing act with the shape. I like mine to be slightly flowy, but petite girls might look like they're drowning if it has too much volume. So make sure yours fits well on the upper body, and then puffs out towards the bottom. And if the colour or print from head to toe feels overwhelming, try adding a belt, worn high around the waist or slung low.

THE SHEATH

When I used to attend mass as a kid with my mom, I noticed most of the stylish women in church wearing these classic fitted dresses that ended just above the knee. I called them 'mass dresses', but let's go with the more popular term: the sheath. The shape suits even curvy women and can be classy or sexy depending on your style. A well-fitted one by McQueen or Zara will also give your bum a lift, so who can complain?

DRESSES

The Must-Haves

THE MINI

In *Kambakkht Ishq*, my size-zero look was all about dangerously short minis, and the look has stayed with me. I love how they make the legs look longer, and, of course, turn any plain Jane into a sexy stunner. I wore a tribal print, sequinned All Saints mini to Karan's fortieth birthday party. It was dangerously short, but it was a huge hit. Picking the right length for yourself really depends on what you're comfortable with, so I would say you have to be the best judge. Just remember, you probably won't be standing the whole time, so pick a style that won't show off too much when you bend over or sit down.

The Must-Have-NOTs!

THE EMPIRE WAISTLINE

Empire waistlines, especially on short girls, just make the figure look stout and heavy. I hadn't consciously thought of it until Tanya pointed it out, but I've never liked myself in this style. It just reminds me of bridesmaid dresses.

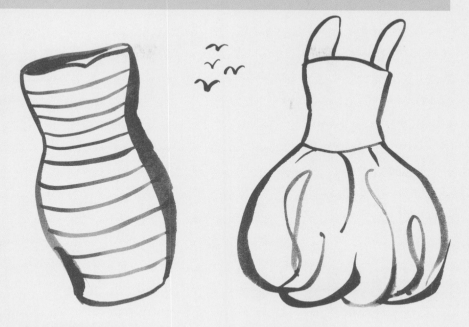

THE BANDAGE

Let's talk about the bandage. It's a classic style, but, somehow, not in India. People here seem to think that wearing a bandage dress will make you seem rich and famous. Breaking news—it doesn't, especially not since everyone and their cousin is now seen wearing the same dress, and doing such a tacky job of it. Every time I turn to page 3 of a newspaper, I see at least two women in bandage dresses. If you have a fabulous body that you've worked hard for and are dying to show off, it's tempting to put on a bandage dress and make all the women in the room jealous. But even if you're dying to be a show-off, you have to wear it differently from the crowd. Throw on a jacket, try a full-length version—just don't let it all hang out.

THE BUBBLE

Every now and then, some evil designer who hates women tries to revive the bubble dress. It's possibly the worst trend I've ever seen in fashion. Except for Crocs. But these puff-pastry dresses just look terrible, especially on women with big calves. No matter what anybody says, I don't think it's flattering on anyone over the age of 12.

Here's my trick to never feeling like a fashion victim. Know exactly what your style is. I call it the 'casual, comfortable' category. If I'm not shooting, my friends and stylists know that my uniform of choice is a tank top, track pants and Havaianas. When I need to dress up, I'm going to reach for that sexy dress with a gorgeous back and a pair of high heels. No confusion, fewer mistakes.

Preppy Princess

You love the combination of crisp white shirts and pleated skirts. You own tonnes of shrugs, sensible jackets and thin sweaters that cover up your arms, and have always had a fascination for oxford shoes. You're not one to be caught wearing leather jackets or bandage dresses. **MUST-HAVE** A sheer white blouse with feminine detailing, paired with a colourful straight-fit pair of pants and a camel tote could be your style signature. **MUST-AVOID** You'll feel completely out of place wearing anything too shimmery or shiny.

Dress Care

My mom taught Lolo and me to separate our clothes into daywear and nightwear, and it's a lesson that's always stayed with me. I hate a messy cupboard, especially since I have so many clothes that I often forget about something for months. Then I suddenly remember if I see a photograph of me wearing it, or find a receipt in a purse.

Here are some wardrobe managing tips I've learnt to save me from losing some favourite, or super-expensive clothes.

Separate your regular day dresses from your more expensive, glamorous cocktail dresses and gowns. Since you'll probably wear the casual clothes more, you don't want to keep pulling out the entire pile to search for just one dress.

Keep your delicate beaded or embroidered dresses in separate bags. This is a tip Manish taught me to take care of his beautiful sheer saris, and I

Off-Screen Sensation

Whatever your favourite actress wears on screen, you have a copy of it in less than a week. When your friends call you filmy, you take that as a compliment, and you know exactly who dresses whom on the red carpet. **MUST-HAVE** No fan of filmi fashion can have a complete wardrobe without a black net sari with red detailing. **MUST-AVOID** Combining too many Bollywood-tribute-looks in one outfit.

Bohemian Babe

Your wardrobe is full of flowing skirts, short kurtis and strong Indian tribal prints. You love wearing kohlapuri chappals and silver jewellery, and never leave the house without loads of kajal. **MUST-HAVE** A tribal-printed maxi dress worn with a braided leather belt, gold kohlapuri chappals and drop earrings would elevate your natural style. **MUST-AVOID** Piling on too many loose layers that make you look shapeless and frumpy.

use it for all my expensive clothes. You never know when a zip or hook from one dress might accidentally latch onto another and rip it. I recently bought a beautiful Catherine Malandrino lace dress that's so dainty I wrapped it in tissue before putting it into a bag to preserve it.

Dresses with stiff pleats or in easily-wrinkled fabrics should be hung, rather than folded. I know that space isn't always available in tiny city apartments, but maybe you could compromise by keeping one tiny section of your cupboard for hanging those precious dresses.

Pack a little bag of potpourri into a section of your wardrobe. I live in Mumbai, and in the monsoon, everything begins to smell musty. Potpourri sachets tucked into different corners keep my clothes smelling fresh and summery, which really makes me want to play dress-up every day.

Sporty Spirit

You feel comfortable in track pants, sweatshirts and running shoes, even when you're not going to the gym. Skirts scare you because you're not comfortable showing off your legs unless you're wearing cycling shorts. And you'd rather have your head shaved than put on a frilly dress. **MUST-HAVE** Racer-back cotton ganji worn with a brightly coloured, fitted jacket over dark-wash jeans strikes the right balance between feminine and fitness freak. **MUST-AVOID** Throwing a sweatshirt on top of everything, no matter what the occasion.

Quirky Queen

You love wearing outfits that can start a conversation, whether it's a jailbird-striped maxi dress or a furry necklace. Your love of colours and crazy prints makes you really stand out in the group, especially when paired with your statement jewellery. **MUST-HAVE** A jacket printed with Indian kitsch iconography worn with shorts, an acrylic necklace and multi-coloured sandals makes you the girl everyone else wants to know. **MUST-AVOID** Piling on so many clashing designs that you look like a printer attacked you.

Classic Chic

You never wear more than three colours at one time, and your wardrobe is full of whites, beiges, blacks and blues. You prefer long sleeves and pencil skirts and will never buy anything that's a trend started by an actress or singer. Anything you own could be worn five years later and seem just as fresh and new. **MUST-HAVE** A floral-printed blazer worn over a cream knee-length dress with a pop-coloured heel adds a little fun to your conservative sensibilities. **MUST-AVOID** Going totally neutral: there's a danger of your disappearing into the background!

THE NINE-TO-FIVE SENSATION

There's a popular myth associated with the Kapoor khandan. Everybody thinks that the women of my family weren't allowed to work after marriage, and that my father was against Lolo and me joining the industry. What rubbish! Papa has always been very proud that his daughters are both strong and independent women who are taking the family tradition forward. I may not discuss work with him and ask for his advice all the time, but he's very supportive of my decisions. And like any other dad, he loves talking about his kids and their achievements. When we inaugurated the Bollywood Walk of Stars in Mumbai together, I think he couldn't have been prouder of the fact that it was his little Bebo, and not any of the Kapoor men, who was picked to represent the family. Cinema runs in our blood, and even my grandfather Raj Kapoor, whose statue we unveiled that day, would have been happy to see me where I am today.

My mom, as all our friends say, is cooler than both her daughters. She worked very hard when we were young to give us a good life, and she knows the importance of being financially independent. My mom has always made sure both her daughters understood the value of professionalism and hard work with no excuses. Whatever else I have been called, being unprofessional is the one thing no one can ever accuse

Even when we're out doing regular stuff like partying or heading to the airport, people are constantly looking at us and forming perceptions. If I step out of the house in a see-through blouse and hot shorts, I'll be ripped apart by the media the very next day. There really is no such thing as personal space when you have photographers following your every move. It gets more intense when I have a movie coming up. Imagine joining a new job every few months, and having to buy a whole new wardrobe to suit your new office. That's what my life feels like.

When I was promoting *Bodyguard*, I dressed like a small-town, stylish Punjabi girl every time I stepped out of the house. Colourful chikan kurtas with patiala pants, tons of bright chudis and simple Kolhapuri chappals became my uniform. Then for *Ek Main Aur Ekk Tu*, I was supposed to look like cool, funky Rhiana Braganza from Las Vegas for all public events. So out went the kurtas and bangles and in came the chunky jewellery, skinny jeans and high heels. I couldn't wear a Lucknowi salwar suit to a press conference even if I wanted to.

Though my job is not exactly a nine-to-five corporate desk job, the rules are pretty much the same. Dress appropriately, leave your attitude at home and be on time. There's absolutely no excuse for dressing badly, especially if you have the basics in your wardrobe.

me of. Mom was more hands-on with Lolo's career initially, going to the sets and making sure that she was taken care of. But by the time I decided to join the industry, Mom knew that I wasn't going to be forced into doing anything I didn't want to do. I was always the headstrong, confident one. Or overconfident, as Mom would sometimes say. Even when I had to wear a bikini in *Tashan*, she was totally fine with it. Her only worry was that I was losing my Bebo curves!

And while people think our life is all glamour and glitz, like any other working woman, actresses also follow dress codes on the job. Actually, we have to be more particular than anyone else.

Interview Ensembles

If you want to impress the boss and get that job, remember that first impressions are everything.

When I was first starting out in films and had to go to script readings, I'd make sure that I was dressed for the part, literally. If the role required me to be a sweet, naive college girl, I'd choose a T-shirt and jeans or a simple salwar kurta, rather than some couture brand. Even models will tell you that when they go for auditions, they need to dress high fashion to convince the judging panel they can pull off runway clothes.

Apart from being punctual and well-mannered, the way you look also says a lot about your personality:

- Bold colours = confidence, go-getter attitude.
- Crisp navy jacket with silk lining and vintage enamel brooch = orderly, attention to detail.
- See-through chiffon blouse = wrong kind of job!

The most important thing to keep in mind is the dress code. If the office environment is very formal, dress conservatively without being too boring, with tailored jackets, wide-legged pants, flowing blouses and fitted sheaths. Alternatively, you can rarely go wrong in a simple cotton sari worn with a well-fitted blouse. Don't let your clothes distract from your intelligence and drive, so no plunging necklines and too-tight skirts, ladies.

If you're feeling comfortable, you'll probably look confident. Keep those sky-high heels for a cocktail party; you'd rather go in sensible wedges or low pumps so you won't be dying of pain with every step you take. If it's summer, choose a dark-coloured ensemble in a light fabric for maximum ventilation. Sweat patches are never a plus point on your CV.

No matter how conservative or boring your office dress code may be, you should always have something on that makes you stand out of the crowd. A brightly coloured scarf, an interesting brooch, or even a signature perfume could help the people in charge remember you as being different from everybody else they met.

Workwear Wardrobe

Being a woman in the workplace is a bit tricky. Guys can get away with wearing the same shirt–trousers combo every single day for the rest of their lives, and nobody will judge them, or care. We need to be a little more careful because having so many choices gives us more room to make mistakes.

In an Indian work environment, going the traditional way never hurts. You can wear colourful kurtas with stretch churi pants or draped patiala pants for a naturally feminine look. Sticking to breathable fabrics like cotton, linen and chiffon is probably best for the weather, and, of course, avoiding too much bling. The silhouette should be simple and elegant so that you can move easily and remain comfortable throughout the day. Indian brands like W, Anokhi and Fab India make the perfect ethnic office wear for women, and are easily available all over the country. I'm sure you'll find plenty of local boutiques in your area, if you're looking for something unique. Even while accessorizing, avoid the temptation to pile on too much jewellery, especially bangles and anklets. The constant noise can be very distracting.

If you prefer western silhouettes, sticking to neatly-tailored shirts and pants in the office is the safest route. You can add variety to your wardrobe by playing with colours, styles and fabrics, as long as transparent and revealing are out of your vocabulary. In more formal environments, draw the line at sleeveless tops, and make sure your skirt doesn't go more than two inches above the knee. I like pencil skirts because they are the perfect balance of conservative and chic. Pair them with a peasant blouse and 2-inch heels, and you'll be the belle of the boardroom.

Hair and Make-Up

I'm a firm believer in keeping your make-up as minimal as possible. Covering your face with product is such a bad idea in our weather; you are not only clogging your pores with chemicals, but there's also a good chance that the heat will make your make-up run and you'll start looking like a melting wax statue. The more make-up you wear, the less natural you look. So don't think you're fooling anybody. Especially when it comes to work, you don't want to look like you're ready to paint the town red!

Keep your daily **MAKE-UP ROUTINE** to the basic three: kajal, mascara, lipstick. I absolutely love lining my eyes with kajal. It makes the puffiness under the eyes seem less prominent, and makes you look chirpy and fresh.

MASCARA will open out your eyes even more and make them pop. But make sure it's not thick and clumpy or you'll have sticky black deposits in the corners of your eyes in no time. Two strokes on the lashes, and you'll be fine.

LIPSTICK should ideally be in a light colour for the day. Try and go for a colour that's closest to your natural lip colour. I personally prefer tinted lip balms.

If you feel you're looking a little pale or under the weather, make an exception and add just **A TINY BIT OF BLUSH** on the apples of your cheeks. A cheek tint is not too high-maintenance, and is also easy to apply. The colour boost will instantly perk you up.

As far as your hair goes, early morning can be a rush but don't push off to work with wet hair. **BLOW-DRY** it enough so it's dry and set! Nothing says inefficient as much as tardiness!

Pull your hair back into a **TIGHT PONYTAIL**. It's fuss-free and keeps your hair maintained and off your face. And looks super slick with a nice business suit.

Keep your **HAIR STYLED**. Get yourself a nice cut so you can maintain it well. No one wants a mess at work!

Job Essentials

1 A Sturdy Carry-All

This is a working woman's survival tool. I personally like massive leather totes that can fit my whole world, and have dozens of little pockets and compartments inside so I don't have to dig through the whole bag to find my stuff. I also like ones which have both shorter handles and a long strap, so I can switch between carrying it on my arm and shoulder. Yves Saint Laurent and Prada are my current go-to bags, though most people in India seem to have a fondness for Louis Vuitton and the Hermès Birkin. Balenciaga's bags are always the coolest of the season, but they're maddeningly expensive too. Indian brands like Lavie make reasonably priced bags too, or you can always hit the high-street and check out brands like Zara and Mango for trendy, yet affordable options.

Your bag must be large enough to accommodate the following:

WALLET Invest in a good one; it's most unimpressive when a shabby wallet is pulled out of an exquisite bag. Plus, always ensure that your wallet has space enough for the 3 c's: cards, cash and change!

CELL PHONE, LAPTOP OR TABLET, KINDLE, IPOD, CHARGERS and other technological innovations that you cannot function without. Don't overdo the technology in your bag. You don't want to break your back lugging this around. So pick and choose carefully. And don't become an office drudge: get yourself some good-looking tech!

MAKE-UP CASE that can carry your essentials! Kajal, mascara, a lipper and a hair brush—for that last minute touch-up before an unexpected work lunch or post-6 p.m. meeting!

WET WIPES Don't raise your eyebrows yet, just hear me out. In our tropical climate, dust, sweat and grease are as unavoidable as Mumbai's traffic jams. Wet wipes can be used to give you a 2-second face refresher, clean your hands after eating greasy snacks or even wipe off a gravy stain. I love face wipes, which I use to take off make-up because I'm just too lazy to wash my face. I know some friends who use Johnson's baby wipes because they're mild on the skin and smell divine. There are even herbal ones, if you prefer organic products.

MINI PERFUME Carrying around your 100 ml bottle of perfume will make your bag weigh a tonne. And God forbid you're taking an especially-bumpy cab ride and it breaks! I like to carry vials of my favourite perfume in my purse or bag, so I never have to worry about smelling less than fabulous at all times. BO is a strict No-No in my book, ladies.

SUNGLASSES for those trips in between meetings. My favourite styles can be found at Prada, Tom Ford and Miu Miu.

SNACK BOX You'll always find a bit of food in my bag, be it peanuts or some fruit. Remember you still want to snack healthy even between nine-to-five.

2 A Well-Fitted Jacket For All Occasions

It doesn't matter if you're a DJ, heart surgeon or history teacher. There will be an occasion when you'll need to wear a jacket, and you do not want to be a grown woman borrowing one from a friend. Invest in a basic colour like black, navy blue, white or grey that can be worn over many different outfits. There's nothing like getting one custom-made for your body from your tailor. But MaxMara and Ralph Lauren make really classy jackets that can be casual or formal depending on how you style them. Wear one with a simple scarf for a client meeting, or toss it over a silk cocktail dress with heels for your annual party. I also like basic jackets from Zara and Mango, which work for smaller budgets. For an Indian touch, Ritu Kumar, Ashish Soni and Annamika Khanna make embroidered bolero jackets, which could become your signature look. Remember a jacket is all about the fit; so when you're buying a ready-made jacket, make sure it fits you like a glove!

3 A Classy Ethnic Outfit

Most women my age avoid wearing saris to work, because it can be quite time-consuming to drape one properly every day. But I think your wardrobe is incomplete without having at least one special Indian garment, either a churidar or sari, that you can wear to occasions like the Diwali party, or a special conference. I think Indian women look most beautiful in the sari, and an elegant one makes you look sensual yet traditional. You could even wear a Manish Malhotra style anarkali kurta with churi pants for a unique look.

THE RED-CARPET ICON

According to my mother the secret of leading a good life is to surround yourself with people who make you happy! My version is: to lead a fashion-fabulous life, surround yourself with people who can make you happy! All those red-carpet appearances and glam photo shoots, including the thirty magazine covers that I did in 2008, involved a lot of team effort from some really bright and fantastic people. All I have to do is turn up on time and look pretty.

I remember shooting for the cover of *Grazia*'s third anniversary issue in 2011. We had only three hours to wrap it all up, which in Bollywood or even the fashion world, is not a lot of time

at all. Most actresses take three hours just sitting in their vanity van getting ready. I had never met the stylist before nor did I know what kind of look they wanted for the shoot. But when I saw one of my favourite photographers R. Burman there, I knew I could kick my feet back and relax. His pictures are and have always been superb anyway. So I let the experts do their job. They showed me a few gorgeous outfits, including the white Dolce & Gabbana dress that finally wound up on the cover. I'll be honest; I didn't think it would work at first. But the stylist was convinced, so I thought, 'What's the harm in trying it out?' I wore the dress, and it was perfect. Sweet, playful and girlie, just

dressing room and down the stairs, I had to fight the urge to wipe it off with a tissue paper. But it worked like a charm, just like the Dolce & Gabbana dress, and I had a lot of positive comments for my look that day.

What I'm trying to say is if you're asking for someone's help, it's important to let them do their job. Being an actress, it's very easy for me to say 'No!' to everything and still get away with it. Trust me, many do. But there's never been room for tantrums in the Kapoor household.

Of course, that doesn't mean I'm going to let them convince me to wear thigh-high boots and a leather corset. I still make stylists stitch up slits that are showing a little too much leg because I'm an Indian girl and I'm just not comfortable with it. But if you trust people and put yourself in their hands, they'll work extra hard to make sure they don't let you down. You'll learn new things from the people around you every day and discover a side of you that you didn't know existed! It's walking a tight rope between expert advice and your individual style. And I think especially when it comes to glamming up, you need a bit of both.

like me. And lucky for us, everybody loved the photos. It got such a great response and *Filmfare* took one of the pictures and put it on their front page. Now that's killing two covers with one shoot!

The same goes with dressing for the red carpet. Before I met my stylist, Tanya Ghavri, I would never have worn red lipstick except for a photo shoot. I'm more of an eye-make-up girl, obsessed with smoky eyes. And I was convinced if I tried wearing both red lipstick and dark eyeshadow, I'd look like a vampire. But Tanya literally fought with me every day until I agreed to wear it to the Apsara Awards. Even until the last minute, right before walking out of my

Since everyone does not have a team of people working to put together that perfect outfit, I have put together all I know, have observed and learnt from one red-carpet appearance to the next so you can find your perfect look!

COUTURE, GLAMOUR AND POISE...

Perfect Your Red Carpet Look in 9 Steps!

1 RSVP Right

My usual routine before a major red-carpet appearance involves a lot of prepping and preening. It's almost like preparing for an exam. First things first: I call my stylist, Tanya, and my style guru, Manish. I then give them a detailed account of what the event is, what the crowd is going to be like and what the mood should be. We make copious notes. I don't usually have too many demands. Just that it has to be fresh, reflect my independent style and be A-MA-ZING!

Here are some things you could do to get yourself the right fashion advice:

• Since everyone doesn't have a stylist I recommend you find yourself your go-to fashion buddy. There's always that one friend who has immaculate taste and who can understand you and help you figure your style out! And if you can't find this friend, fashion magazines and the Internet is always a backup.

• What you need to get right before you begin hunting for your perfect look is nailing the dress code; depending on the occasion you neither want to be too understated or OTT. So how glam do you want to go?

• You definitely want to consider the venue. Is it indoors or outdoors? Also take into consideration the weather and ambience of the event.

• You also need to picture what kind of impact you want to create when you make your big entrance! That will take you one step closer to figuring out the kind of outfit you will be scouting for.

• Take notes throughout. Thinking about all of this will lead you nowhere. You need it written in ink for later reference!

2 R&D!

This is the part I usually wriggle my way out of: research! Manish and Tanya go mad chasing down references for the perfect look. I was never really fond of homework, so I'm glad I have them to do this for me. They look through magazines and designer collections online and basically hunt for the best-looking outfit they can find. We then sit together and choose what works and settle on a few options, creating a shortlist of sorts.

Yes, yes, I know everyone isn't lucky enough to have Manish Malhotra on speed dial! So here's what you need to do:

- Get fashion educated: *Vogue, Harper's Bazaar, Cosmopolitan* and *Grazia* are going to become your new best friends! Look out for fashion trends of the season but don't become a fashion victim. Look for styles you like and not for fads you like! Rip pages off, go online and print out looks you like.

Whether you're prepping for that big anniversary celebration, your company's annual Diwali bash or the hottest New Year's party in the city, here's your own do-it-yourself guide to making sure all eyes are on you.

- If you're looking to indulge, get off your ass and into designer stores and browse for a whole weekend before you begin shortlisting your options. Take that fashion-friendly friend of yours. An extra pair of eyes always helps! Remember: no shopping, just window shop, so you know the styles and rates out there.
- Sit and shortlist. Create a list of outfits you like that are suitable for the occasion you're planning on attending!

TRICK!

Here's something you can keep in mind even when there's no occasion round the corner: if you find yourself browsing through a magazine or catalogue and something catches your eye, tear it out. Use the camera on your phone when you're strolling through a mall or generally window-shopping; even if you're not going to buy it then and there, click and save it. Create your own lookbook. So when an occasion strikes you have your own scrapbook of references to go through!

3 The Look!

Tanya and Manish know exactly what flatters my body. They know exactly how to highlight my curves and my colour right! As you know, I love an outfit that can show off my back and bum! Because Tanya loves getting me to try new styles, she brought over four different gowns for the *Agent Vinod* premier. One was a gorgeous mermaid gown, another had a sexy Dolce & Gabbana-ish corset top half, the third was a halter-dress with a super hot low back and finally, there was a really delicate flowy gown. Can you imagine what torture it was picking just one? Each deserved its own red carpet—I even thought of convincing Saif to have four different premieres, but he'd think I had gone mad. So instead I got him to pick! In fact, I usually parade all the clothes for Saif, just to see which one makes him smile the widest. And he's got perfect taste, so we hardly ever disagree. Ladies, I say get your man to give his opinion too. My job is easy—keep trying on outfits, and pick the one he likes the most. It's like having my own private fashion show with me as the star.

But I digress. Coming back to your look now, after all the research you now know your options. Now you want to figure out the general elements of your look. Sequins vs satin? Thigh-high vs ankle-skimming? Form-fitting vs fluid and flirty? You need to find a look that best suits your body frame and personality.

So here are a few pointers . . .

- Tall, skinny girls can wear floor-length gowns without a problem.
- Shorter women might want to stick with a higher hemline so that you can show off a bit of leg to lengthen the frame.
- If you have a toned body, you could try something a little body-conscious. And show off those legs and arms.
- Curvier girls should opt for draped dresses that glide gently over their problem areas. Drapes can give you an hourglass figure if worn right.
- Choosing a colour palette other than black is always a good idea, because you can be guaranteed there'll be at least ten other women there wearing similar dresses.
- Another avoidable colour is red! I know it's my lucky colour but not on the red carpet. What's the point in spending that much time and effort if you're going to blend into the background. I don't mind wearing red dresses to a regular party or an event, but nowhere where I'll match with the furnishing.

4 Shopping!

This is my absolute favourite part! I must admit, though, these days I barely get a chance to actually go shopping for each event. Tanya usually does this bit for me, so I miss out on a lot of the fun! But lucky for me they get what I want absolutely right almost every time. And getting into those gorgeous dresses almost makes up for the missed shopping expeditions. But this is the trickiest part. After squeezing in and out of a dozen dresses, if you still haven't found 'the one', you're definitely going to be your crabby best!

Here are a couple of things to keep in mind for a great shopping experience:

- An easy way to beat the fashion fatigue is to take **a couple of friends** along to boost your spirits and give you an honest opinion.
- Even before you step out of your house, zone in on your **budget** and make a list of the shops that you know will give you plenty of options to choose from. That way, you won't have to break the bank, or your head, in order to find the perfect dress. Remember the window shopping from earlier: this is where your handy shortlist comes into play!
- A helpful tip is to always carry a pair of **heels** along, so that you know exactly how it's going to look when you actually step out on D-Day. You need to get your frame and length right.
- Don't forget to **move around** in the

trial room. Remember that you're not going to be standing in one place like a statue on the night of the party, and so your dress needs to be comfortable enough for you to walk, skip, sit and jump in. If it's not easy to wear in the store, imagine what a nightmare it will be when you really need it.

- Ensure your **lingerie** is right for the dress. Else that should be next on your list and in your budget. There's nothing worse than a visible panty line or a nip-slip fiasco!
- When you're dressing in the light of your bedroom or even a trial room for that matter, you can't really judge how sheer a dress is going to be. Especially if, like me, you have to pose for a lot of photographs, you might want to check if your lace dress needs a little extra lining. **Step outside**; sunlight's usually the best judge!
- Avoid impulse buying. I'm pretty impulsive myself so I know exactly how silly some of your buys can be—trust me, I have a very embarrassing corner in my wardrobe which is living proof of this! Try it on and **be absolutely sure** before you pick the outfit up.

5 Trial and Error!

Once the dresses are sourced, we have the prelims or, as the fashion people call it, fittings. We try and do this at least a week or so before a major event. Why do we need that much time? Well, because fashion designers love making clothes for super-skinny, super-tall fashion models, and I'm still a foot away from being the next Gisele Bundchen. So we have to make adjustments. Usually shortening the hem and taking the back in or some such. So the dress looks like it was actually made for and on me. Whether your dress is custom-designed or off the rack, ensure you get it fitted to perfection.

TRICK!

Try it on and let them mark and pin the dress on you for best results!

6 Accessorize!

Once you've got the dress in the bag, it's time to focus on accessories. Don't be afraid to go stark, because minimal will always be stylish. But if you feel you need a little extra icing on this cake, shoes, bags and accessories are next on the menu. The entire ensemble needs attention to detail.

When Tania and I make our selections, we pair a few options against the dress and pick the one that we like most. If the dress already has a lot of embellishment on it, you might want to tone down the accessories. I'm personally not a big fan of jewellery dripping from every limb; it's more about a single statement item like a stunning necklace or earrings for me.

Shoes are also very important, because they can really elevate an outfit, or drag it down completely. Open-toed pumps or strappy sandals are usually your safest bet, and if you're going to be standing or dancing all night, you might want to consider a heel that's not too high. No sense in risking an ankle injury just to look good for the first 10 minutes.

The clutch is a definite must-have. Over-sized envelope versions are hot these days, though a classic minaudière never goes out of style. Remember you need enough space to carry your phone, credit card, money and make-up essentials in one place.

TRICK!

I picked this up during my boarding school days, when we were always told to keep a needle and thread handy, just in case you need to stitch up a button that pops off in the middle of a party. Since I haven't touched a needle in years, and will probably end up poking myself, I think safety pins can do just as well. So always carry that safety pin to avoid that dreaded wardrobe malfunction.

7 Beautify!

After we've settled on the shoes and accessories, my make-up and hair team usually zip into action. Sometimes, the dress is perfect, but the hair and make-up can totally let you down. I'm obsessed with my long straight hair, and usually avoid doing anything too experimental to it. But if the dress demands it, like if it has a lovely bejewelled neckline that I can show off, I'll opt for a pretty chignon or a side plait. Decide on what you're doing with your hair and face in advance: you don't want to be wiping out make-up and reapplying it an hour before you have to leave. Plus, you might want to have your hair done earlier! So always be prepared.

Here are a few things to keep in mind to make your beauty session as easy as possible.

- Your look should always complement an outfit, never clash with it. So if there's a lot going on with your dress—patterns, prints, colours, textures—keep the make-up dialled down.
- On more subtle outfits, you can play with the face paint. Maybe try an eye-popping lipstick, or bright colour on the eyelids. But whatever you do, don't wear both at the same time.
- A nice colour on the lips, a little blush and loads of kajal and mascara on the eyes is my tried-and-tested success formula.

- A word of advice: spend a little money on make-up that's transfer- and water-resistant, or you'll be leaving smudges and stains everywhere.
- Make-up is usually applied before I wear my outfit, so that nothing drops on to the designer clothes. But if your dress is one of those super-fitting varieties that you have to pull over your head, put it on, cover up with a towel or robe, and then get started on your make-up.
- The hair is always a tricky situation, because it depends completely on the kind of outfit you're wearing. If you've got a lovely neckline and want to show it off, it's nice to put the hair up into a chic chignon or bring it over to one side in a sexy side plait.
- It might actually be a good idea to practice the hairstyle in advance if you're doing it yourself, because you don't want to be struggling with your hair at the last minute.
- And when in doubt, a bouncy blow-dry usually suits most outfits perfectly.
- Get to the salon a day in advance; you don't want your skin all inflamed and teased on the day itself.
- Manicure, pedicure, waxing, facial and a full-body massage just to pamper yourself is a must before a grand function!

8 D-Day

The good thing is it usually takes me very little time to dress up on the day because so much preparation has already gone into it. Not that nothing ever goes wrong. There's always the possible disaster of having a zip break or a stain suddenly appear out of nowhere. But I haven't had a wardrobe malfunction so far, so I guess the planning helps. So keep everything ready and then just slip from one thing into the next, till your shoes are on and you're ready to step out! And after all that effort, the best results are seeing the look being discussed over and over in the newspapers and fashion magazines and on blogs. Or finding out that women are taking pictures of the dress to their tailors and asking for copies. Dolce & Gabbana won't be happy, but I think it's sweet. You know what they say: imitation is the best form of flattery!

9 The Grand Entrance!

Fashion is about having fun with your wardrobe, and nothing is more fun than dressing up for a night out. Ever wondered why celebrities always manage that spectacular entrance? Because we practice! All my friends tease me saying that I'm a complete drama queen, especially when it comes to getting ready for an important event. I like practicing my pose in front of the mirror, figuring out my best angles. I fully recommend you try it. It just puts you in a good mood for the rest of the night.

• Spend a bit of time in front of the mirror.

Make up your mind about **your attitude** for the night.

• **Posture and poise are key**. Walk around a bit, even sit, stand and talk to yourself. As long as you're comfortable you'll be a star.

• That's also the secret to getting yourself clicked right! Don't be afraid to **try out a few poses** in front of your mirror at home, especially if you are going to be taking a lot of photos that night. Who knows where those pictures are going to land up; and you don't want to be the girl who had her eyes closed in every one.

5 Minutes To Perfection

But what happens if you don't have a fortnight to prepare and land up with a last-minute invite? With the number of appearances and event invitations, there are many last-minute do's I have had to attend. No preparation, no day at the salon, nothing! But don't worry; you can still look absolutely fab! Trust me, I've done it a million times. So here's my quick-fix solution for those forgotten and last minute invites; just follow this basic checklist and rock the party:

• First things first: the **outfit**! Go back to the basics. You have two options here. Get that trusty pair of dress jeans and dress it up with a nice top. Or if you have that LBD sitting in your wardrobe, now's the time to grab it.

• Dress your outfit up with a stunning statement **necklace** or large dangler **earrings** for instant glamour. Remember this is an either/or. Do not overload on the jewellery. You don't want to try too hard.

• **Eyeliner and mascara** can really lift even the most basic look. They make your eyes come alive and add a much-needed sense of drama.

• **Heels, heels, heels**. The higher, the better. I usually go for 6-inch stilettos for the full diva effect, and trust me, it can really make heads turn.

• **A big smile** is really your best accessory. If you're not having fun, even a custom-made Valentino gown will lose its charm.

Posture and poise are key. As long as you're comfortable you'll be a star.

COUTURE, GLAMOUR AND POISE...

Favourite Red-Carpet Designers

One of the best red-carpet designers is Elie Saab. I've worn his lovely shimmery gowns on so many occasions and they've always been a hit. His designs always make me feel elegant and glamorous. He somehow manages to create the most comfortable outfits! So Elie Saab remains my most obvious option.

Roberto Cavalli is for when I want to go all out and be a proper diva. The gowns are always so sexy and flattering to the body that they make you look and feel like a goddess. Plus, he designs for curvy girls, which deserves a huge thumbs up according to me.

Dolce & Gabbana makes chic eye-catching gowns that nobody can ignore. They're also the gods of corsets, and if you're ever feeling bloated around the tummy, this is the brand that will come to your rescue.

Armani Prive is a label that is loved by everyone, including all the Hollywood stars, for its chic look and classic cuts. I think Giorgio Armani is a genius, and his clothes always make me feel like a superstar.

Vivienne Westwood is such a fun label, and for good reason. Even her simplest designs are like something from a mad dream, so you know that every rupee you're paying is worth it.

A new favourite, Paule Ka is a French label that makes really simple, but really elegant gowns that really suit my figure. They do a lot of designs in my favourite pastel colours like lavender, blush pink and baby blue.

Among the Indian designers, it's no secret that Manish Malhotra is my go-to man. He's really the best at mixing traditional Indian aesthetic with a touch of sex appeal and glamour. More importantly, he's one of my closest friends and really understands what I like. So I feel completely safe when he's in the room. People accuse me of being a Manish Malhotra brand ambassador, and I must admit I cannot get enough of him!

But there are a few other labels that I'm beginning to like too. I recently wore a Masaba Gupta sari to an event, and it was so different from what I usually wear that it actually made me feel like a new person.

I also like the dresses that Rohit Gandhi & Rahul Khanna make with their label Cue. Their clothes look very international with lots of attitude, and they're trendy without trying too hard.

Namrata Joshipura also makes some fab gowns, which I discovered after wearing a full- length, black sequinned and feathered one to an event. It actually fit me perfectly the first time I put it on. I'm glad someone is designing clothes for the voluptuous Indian woman. Thank you, Namrata!

COUTURE, GLAMOUR AND POISE...

Gown Guide

BACKLESS I'm not into plunging necklines. I keep telling my stylist, 'Listen, it can't be so low,' and she'll say, 'But in *Chameli*, your sari blouses were cut so low.' But that was a film, and of course I can't wear revealing necklines out in public. My mom will kill me! But that doesn't mean I like the high-collared Victorian-style necks either. Like with all curvy women, high necks don't work on me. I have a feeling that it makes me look shorter, and so I feel suffocated if anything goes higher than my collar bones. So while I'm not going to take the plunge, I definitely like a bit of breathing space! What I'm perfectly OK with is a backless dress. I have a pretty nice back and I don't mind showing it off. If Lolo and I are dressing up together to go out, she'll go through my cupboard and say, 'I can't even find one thing that I could wear.' She's always looking for something high-necked and full-sleeved, and I'm always picking out the most daring gowns. I've tried convincing her that she's got such a stunning figure that she should show it off.

STRAPLESS Tube gowns are a bit of a controversy. Sometimes, they look great, like the Blumarine gown I wore to the *GQ* awards, but other times, they may emphasise my arms. Generally, I think they look good on women who have well-defined collar bones and slim arms. Also, since you have to wear a strapless bra, which means less support, it's probably not the best style for heavy-chested women.

HALTER The halter is a classic and usually looks good on every body type. There's another opportunity to show off the back, so obviously I love it. But if you're wearing one with bejewelled straps, avoid wearing any jewellery around the neck. That's a little too over-the-top.

MERMAID Mermaid gowns, which are narrow till the knee before puffing out again, make your butt look fantastic. They give you a perfect hourglass shape. Though, it's a dramatic shape, so wear it with confidence or it'll seem like a costume. They're also slightly difficult to walk in. That's why comfortable shoes are important.

TRICK! When in doubt, wear a sari! The sari is truly timeless. It's the sexiest combination of being fully covered and yet showing a hint of skin. The true Indian body type looks great in a sari, so whoever invented it was a genius. And I haven't yet come across a body type it doesn't suit. Obviously, if I'm going with an Indian look, then I'll pick a lace or net sari. When it comes to the sari blouse, I don't like it when the blouse cuts into my arms. I prefer wearing blouses that are long-sleeved or completely sleeveless. Now a lot of designers have started making sheer sleeves with delicate embroidery on them, which can look really lovely. Even today, though I love wearing all the top international brands, I'm most comfortable in my Manish Malhotra net sari. It's become my signature style. But more on this later ...

THE DESI STUNNER

So, what do I do if I can't decide which of the ten gowns my stylists picked out I like the most? I drop the dresses and pick up a sari instead!

I honestly feel safest in ethnic clothes. From kurtas and saris to lehengas and patiala suits, they tick all the right boxes: sexy, comfortable, feminine, elegant and body-flattering. Not to mention Indian clothes are like Dr Fixit for all your body issues. No matter what you think your problem is, there's something here to solve it. Put on a little weight? A sweeping anarkali with a low back worn over a slim churidar promises to reveal only as much as you want to. Dream of having an hourglass figure? Your wish has been granted, thanks to the bust-enhancing choli, and smartly draped folds of a sari. No wonder all Hindi movie heroines chose their chiffons over bikinis!

Even on screen, some of my most loved looks have been totally desi. I

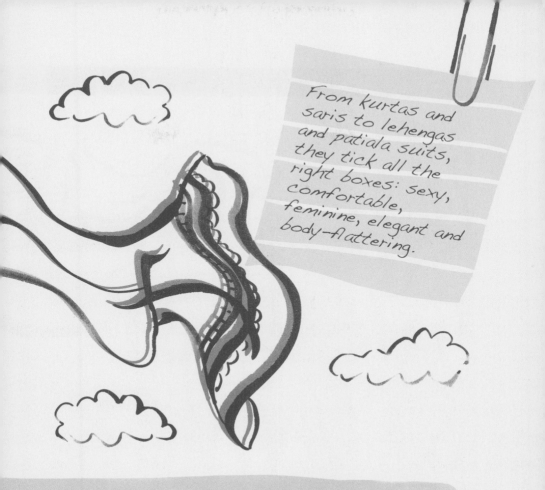

From kurtas and saris to lehengas and patiala suits, they tick all the right boxes: sexy, comfortable, feminine, elegant and body-flattering.

read in a newspaper that after my mujra performance in *Agent Vinod*, orders for shararas went through the roof. It was a style that had almost been forgotten in mainstream fashion, but overnight it was revived and became the coolest style to wear to a wedding. The ladies of my mom's generation understood the power of desi style, so it always makes me smile when I see a young woman choose an elegant sari over a wrap dress, and make it completely her own.

And thanks to the hours of handcrafted work put in by our gifted craftsmen, they're works of art. Most of these techniques of weaving, embroidering and dyeing are so rare that big international designers have been coming to India for years to learn from us. Even the God of shoes, Christian Louboutin, admits that India and its creative arts are his inspiration. What more convincing do you need?

The Sari

The best thing about saris is that they never really go out of style. Even the old silk saris that my mom has so lovingly wrapped in mal and saved for me are now like beautiful vintage pieces, almost like heirlooms. My designer gowns cost an arm and a leg, but they barely last more than a couple of months. After two wears, I find holes in them, and I have no idea how that happened.

Saris have always been my comfort dressing. It is the simplest clothing concept in the world: just six yards of cloth draped over your body. But it has the power to transform you from a sweet girl next door into an elegant goddess within a matter of seconds. In fact, when everybody else had suddenly discovered gowns and were wearing them to red-carpet events like they were going out of style, I decided to go desi. I still remember the fuss my black net sari with red embroidery kicked up a few years ago. It was all over the Internet and in every fashion magazine. I think the few other versions that Manish made for his label were sold out before they even hit the shelves.

That's how the net sari became my signature, a classic style with just the right amount of modern sex appeal. In fact, if I wear anything other than a gorgeous drape to the *Filmfare* awards, my fans actually get upset. Even my stylists agree, 'You can wear gowns everywhere else, but for *Filmfare*, it has to be a sari.'

And how could I say anything about my favourite saris without mentioning the *Chammak Challo* look. For an Indian housewife, which was my character in the film, that was a pretty daring wardrobe choice. The plunging neckline with the flame red sari draped low on my hips, paired with that waist-chain. Even Shah Rukh said it was the best I've ever looked in a sari. And I agree!

What makes it constantly challenging is that there isn't one standard way to drape it. You could let your imagination run wild and turn and twist it any way you like, as long as you're confident of carrying it off. You don't even have to wear them with a petticoat anymore. I've seen them being paired with flared pants and tight churis too, but that's a look that I'm just not ready for yet.

The 5 Must-Have Saris

THE NET SARI Let's just agree that I'm the brand ambassador of net saris. It's a complete argument killer for anybody who says the sari is too dowdy or old-fashioned. Forget the bandage dress, there's nothing that shows off your figure better than a sheer sari with just the right amount of shimmer or embroidery to give you a dose of glamour. You need to have a super-toned tummy to pull this one off, and, of course, a sexy butt. And as far as designers go, the buck stops at Manish Malhotra.

THE LACE SARI Since lace is such a romantic theme, why not wear it in a sari too. This offers more coverage than the net sari, but has something uniquely feminine and old-world to it. Since it's a thin fabric, it won't add bulk to your body, which is a problem that many women face with silk saris. Suneet Verma is the king of lace saris, and his creations can be passed on from generation to generation.

THE PRINTED COTTON SARI When you're headed out for a stylish brunch where you know everybody else will be wearing white dresses and loose trousers, lead the way in a brightly printed cotton sari. You can drape it in innovative ways to really stand out from the crowd. Masaba Gupta and Anupama Dayal make such fun quirky prints that everybody will be dying to know where you got your outfit from.

THE CHIFFON SARI Maybe it's the Bollywood heroine in me, but I think you can't really have a complete wardrobe without a chiffon sari. It was my grandfather Raj Kapoor who first popularized the idea of women wearing flimsy chiffon saris and dancing around trees and under waterfalls, and that became the icon of Indian sensuality.

THE SILK SARI A silk sari, whether it's a rich Kanjeevaram, a sensuous Chanderi or a luxurious Benarasi, is an heirloom piece that every Indian woman should own. Aamir Khan got me hooked to the Chanderi silk saris because it's a cause close to his heart, and he even gifted me quite a few pieces. In any other country in the world, the words 'silk' and 'handmade' would have people fainting in a fashion frenzy. We're so lucky that it's part of our heritage, and must definitely do our bit to preserve it.

Top Sari Tips

Once you've got the sari in place, you need to accessorize it right. A gorgeous designer sari can be let down by tacky jewellery or a boring sari blouse.

- The sari blouse is where your creativity really shines through, especially if you're getting one custom-designed. Opt for a low back instead of a plunging neckline, or consider a halter-neck if you're confident your pallu will stay in place. You could also go for a choli in a contrasting colour or fabric, if the sari is more neutral. A sequinned or velvet top adds drama to a plain drape.

- Three-quarter sleeves work well for women with slightly pudgy arms, while Lolo looks stunning in strappy blouses showing off her toned arms. Somehow I'm not a big fan of the half sleeve, because it cuts you off at an awkward point, creating two sausages above and below the patti.

- With Indian clothes, you can only wear Indian jewellery. A kundan necklace or a stunning pair of chandelier earrings will really take the style to the next level. Geetanjali makes such beautiful jewellery that I fall in love with all the pieces every time I have to shoot an ad for them. But don't fall prey to the temptation to go on bling-overload. That will only kill the elegance of the sari.

- Since getting the sari length right is important, wear your shoes as you begin draping it. The hemline should show off just a little bit of your toes, which also eliminates the danger of your stepping on your own outfit and falling over on your face!

- If you're wondering what bag matches your sari best for a night out, don't even consider anything other than a clutch. Handbags worn with saris remind me of aunties going to the market.

The Lehenga

It's the ultimate combination of east meets west, even though it's much older than the concept of 'Indian fusion': a short top and a gorgeous panelled skirt, an ingenious combination. I love the drama of twirling around, and letting the skirt lift off the ground like I'm walking on a cloud. They are also exquisitely detailed, and some take months to make if they're hand-embroidered and multi-panelled.

But if you thought that lehengas were easier to walk in than saris, think again. Wedding lehengas, especially, can be very heavy: they often weigh about 10 kilos and more. When I shot for the Geetanjali jewellery ad, I was wearing a Tarun Tahiliani lehenga which was absolutely breathtaking, but carrying it around would have given anyone a quick biceps workout.

But lehengas don't always have to be super-sized. When Saif and I first walked for Manish's show together, he made me a lehenga, but with a twist. Instead of a choli and flared skirt, I wore a backless, draped choli with a sexy velvet A-line skirt. It was so different—cooler than anything I had seen in that style—that it could almost pass off for a desi gown. He had even given it a knee-high slit, so that the slim silhouette wouldn't force me to hobble on the ramp. Aside from being a major hit, it was much easier to walk in than some of the other showstopper outfits I've worn, I can promise you!

If you have a toned stomach, then by all means show it off as the lehenga is one of the few outfits you can wear which exposes your navel but doesn't seem trashy. Another popular style is to have a corset choli. The corset will suck in your stomach, so think of it as worth a hundred crunches. The fun part is in the back, where the criss-cross tie-ups can be designed in such a way that they play peek-a-boo with your back.

A style that's super hot right now with designers is to make the border of the skirt so thick that the lehenga can almost stand on its own like a tent. They're also super voluminous, and can be quite a task to walk in. That's all very dramatic, but it probably only suits tall women who won't seem like they're drowning in it. For more petite girls, I would recommend the slim skirt, like the ramp showstopper I mentioned before. It'll show off your tiny figure, and the slim fit will add height to your frame.

Apart from Manish's designs, I like that Anamika Khanna makes light wearable lehengas that women can move in without feeling weighted down. She also has interesting variations on the choli, even turning them into mini shirts, which is such a bright idea. Tarun's lehengas are like works of art, and each one is so intricately embroidered that I'm almost afraid to touch them, for fear I loosen a thread and the whole thing starts unravelling. Rohit Bal's work is very popular, and when you see his wonderfully creative pieces, you'll know why.

The Desi Suit

After *Jab We Met* reinvented the salwar, *Bodyguard* made the churidar a big hit again. I won't be modest and deny that my films made the whole 'Punjabi kudi' look popular again. While I was promoting *Bodyguard*, I got to wear the most fabulous churidar suits in bright pop colours. Manish claims that the line modelled along the film's look which he created for his stores was sold out before he managed to put up even one piece. Now that's the kind of news I like hearing!

Just like the sari, the churidar is constantly being reinvented. There was a time when the kurta was so short that it just about covered the butt, leaving the legs exposed in tight churi pants. Now, women prefer to wear them almost ankle-length.

Manish himself pioneered the super-voluminous anarkali top that looks like it has a crinoline built under it. If drama is what you love, then this is the style for you.

Pick Your Style

PETITE One advantage is that you can wear a figure-hugging kurta with a low back and nobody can complain. The downside is that you can't wear too much volume, because that'll make it seem like the kurta is wearing you. You can even go for the 1960s-style shorter kurta to show off more leg and create the illusion of being taller. Or an asymmetrical hemline, which goes from being really high on one side to ankle-length on the other, could add a few inches to your height.

CURVY An anarkali kurta that fits until just below the bust, and then flares out gives you the best of both worlds. It shows off the good curves and hides the unwanted ones. You could even get your designer to make one that mimics the wrap-dress effect on the top half, which will slim down your frame even more.

TALL Show off your height with a kurta that reaches almost till mid-calf, with a flare at the bottom to balance out your shoulders. You could even consider adding an extra slit running down the centre, which would detract attention from your body to your miles-long legs.

Churi Check

With the classic Indian suit, the bottom allows you to have as much fun and variety as the kurta. Here's how to get one that best suits your style:

CHURI PANTS in stretch fabrics work for almost all body types. Unless you have a curvy torso and skinny legs, which will then make you look like a lollipop in these. **SALWAR PANTS** are wide and comfortable, which make them everybody's practical bet. But I feel it's a slightly more mature look, so wear them at the risk of seeming a couple of years older than you are. **DHOTI PANTS** are the new cool, and come in soft, supple fabrics that make it seem like you're floating instead of walking. Nikasha Tawadey makes hers in gorgeous pop colours that look almost edible. **CIGARETTE PANTS** in a totally contrasting print, like Masaba Gupta makes them, are the urban, cool take on the traditional salwar kurta. **NUDE LEGGINGS** are certainly not for the faint-hearted, but look super sexy if you have the toned calves to carry them off.

Here Comes the Bride!

Let's face it. When it comes to a big fat noisy wedding, nobody does it better and bigger than us. We actually wear couture, and think nothing of the Rs 2 lakh that we pay for something we may never wear again. And since it's literally like a public fashion show, even if you're not the one getting married, you get to dress up to the hilt and can be sure that every other girl in the room is checking you out. It's always a battle of the Sabyasachis and JJ Valaya's vs the Tarun Tahilianis and Manish Malhotras—until the bride shows up and the spotlight goes over to her. And you lucky lady who's found her Prince Charming, consider this the biggest and most glamorous red-carpet moment of your life. You're the star attraction, so the outfit has to be perfect.

The Sangeet

Here's your chance to showcase your own unique style instead of going totally traditional. It's the Indian version of a bachelorette party. For the bride, this is your last wild night before you settle down, so don't be afraid to show off your cool side. But since you'll want to dance and enjoy yourself, think 'sexy, but light'.

If you're going the traditional route, consider a pre-constructed sari which you basically have to zip up like a dress. It allows you to dance your heart out to *Chammak Challo* without worrying about your pleats coming undone, Draupadi style. Gaurav Gupta, Shane and Falguni Peacock and Shantanu and Nikhil make very modern pre-constructed saris, for brides who really want to rock the dance floor.

I also like the idea of wearing a very daring choli with a rich, voluminous lehenga. Since I'm not big on sequins and heavy stones adding unnecessary weight to my clothes, I'd go with a layered net skirt in a beautiful colour with intricate embroidery. Not only is it very dramatic, but it also makes for gorgeous pictures. Imagine that full skirt twirling around as you dance. Stunning!

Or if you really want to push the envelope, how about a sensual, backless anarkali kurta, worn with sparkly nude leggings. It's a completely different take on the usual fare, and might even send your to-be husband's temperature soaring.

You might even consider wearing a gown for the sangeet, to mix things up. You already know my favourite brands and styles, so finding the right one for your body type should not be too hard. Just one word of caution: since you'll be dancing around so much, look for dresses that offer the right support. Strapless gowns might not be such a good idea, or you'll spend a lot of time pulling your neckline up.

How about a sensual, backless anarkali kurta?

TOP TIPS

If you're not best friends with Manish Malhotra like me, don't panic. Almost every bridal store now has a team of experts to guide you through the maze of designers, fabrics, styles and budgets. Ask the store owner to set you an appointment, and let them show you all they have to offer.

- Stores also offer better deals if you're getting **MORE THAN ONE** outfit designed by them. Find one that has the widest range of things you like, so that you're not running from one place to another on your big day.

- **DO YOUR RESEARCH**. Every girl already has her dream wedding mapped out in her head. So look through magazines, search for references online and spend some time window shopping before you settle on the store or designer you absolutely want.

- **ALWAYS ASK ADVICE** of your recently married friends. Even if what they like is completely different from your own taste, they'll have important contacts, and more importantly, have already done all the research before you.

- Once you've picked out the ideal outfit, **SEND PICTURES** and references to your hair and make-up artists so that they can design looks that will complement the clothes.

Get Rid of Bridezilla!

Your big day can easily turn into the worst day of your life, if you're not prepared for it. And of course, you don't want to go from being the demure dulhan to a screaming, raging bridezilla that everybody's terrified of. Once you've settled on a date, follow this easy step-by-step guide to make sure disaster doesn't strike.

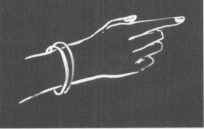

Six Months to the Wedding

- All the best venues in your city will be booked months in advance, so you cannot cross the six-month-deadline if you want to secure your **DREAM LOCATION**. Scout around for the best spots, preferably with your partner, so you both know exactly how many people the hall can accommodate. That way, planning your guest list won't turn into a shouting match. Most places also have their own catering, photography and decorating services, so make sure you get the best deal for your money.

- **IDENTIFY YOUR DESIGNER**. Wedding dresses, especially Indian lehengas and saris, take months to craft if you want yours custom-made. There's also the fittings process, where you have to go back at least three times to make sure every strap sits in place and nothing is too tight or loose. The designer needs time to draw up your ideal look, pick the right fabric, and then get it all together. Oh, and don't forget your husband-to-be. We all know it's your day, but he needs to be dressed for the occasion too.

- Most brides have dreams of being slim and svelte on their big day. But if all my advice has taught you anything, it is that having your **DREAM BODY** doesn't happen overnight. Hit the treadmill with a vengeance and get in touch with a trainer at the gym closest to your house, so that you can't make any excuses. Most places offer special bridal packages which will give you a clear goal to focus on. Take your partner along too! Like the US Army says, 'no man left behind'. If you're already enrolled in a yoga class, inform your instructor that you're planning to get hitched, and she can design a special routine for you. Consulting a dietician will give your exercise regimen a boost, especially if you're very far from your goal weight.

- Draw up a **GUEST LIST**. Trust me, at the last minute, your mom or his will remember some long-lost aunt that they forgot to invite, but who absolutely must attend. The problem will be solved if you have both sides sit down together and decide who they want to see at the wedding. Telling your friends and family casually many months in advance will also allow them to plan their dates, and book tickets to get there if they have to. You don't want your best friend in London cursing you because she has to pay double the airfare, thanks to your late invite!

One Month to the Wedding

- **SEND OUT THE INVITATIONS**. A last-minute wedding card is considered to be insulting, especially in India. People usually expect theirs to be hand-delivered, but not everybody has the time to go from door to door. If you're sending the card to a friend or family member whom you haven't met in a long time, it might be nice to call them just to let them know what to expect in the mail.

- Start shopping for all your wedding day **MUST-HAVES**: shoes, jewellery, special lingerie, make-up, clutch and a change of shoes for when you want to hit the dance floor. Shopping for something specific, even when you don't have a deadline, can be frustrating. So imagine how much worse it gets when your D-Day draws closer by the minute and you can't spot the perfect pair of heels to go with your Manish Malhotra couture lehenga.

- Organize a **FITTING** with your designer. Hopefully, you've come close to your ideal body size now, and if the change has been dramatic, you need to let him or her know. You don't want your expensive one-of-a-kind outfit to be hanging on you like a farmer's overalls.

- Book your **MAKE-UP ARTIST**. Unless you plan to pull a Kate Middleton and do your own make-up, you'll need an expert's help. Solicit recommendations from your just-married friends and check online. I would strongly advise Mickey Contractor for every bride, but talent like that doesn't come cheap.

- Start with your **FACIAL OR SPA TREATMENTS**. Even if you're not a salon junkie, every girl wants to look extra gorgeous on her wedding day. And you need a little time before the results of a facial begin to show. Get yourself a consultation with a good dermatologist or facialist, and let them design a therapy that works for your skin specifically. Two or more sittings before your big day will give you an authentic bridal glow.

One Week to Go

- Here's where you stop being a control freak and start **DESIGNATING JOBS** to a close group of family and friends you can trust. Put your best friend in charge of decorations, your uncle in charge of managing the bar and ask your sister to help with the guests. If you try and manage everything on your own, you'll have dark circles and a nervous tic by the time you get to the actual wedding day.

- Check on the **VENUE, CATERERS AND PHOTOGRAPHERS**, so that there are no last-minute goof-ups. You don't want to be the girl whose party was ruined because the hall was double-booked.

- Finish your **LAST FITTING** with your designer. Some people leave this literally to the eve of their wedding. I don't know how that's even possible, and wouldn't want to imagine what they'd do if something went wrong. Doing it a week in advance gives you a little room to get the designer to adjust the choli or fix a problem with the embroidery. Any less time than that and you're just asking for trouble.

- Try and organize at least one **MEETING** between all the key members of your family and his. This will give you time to discuss last-minute changes, and basically bring everybody up to speed.

- And finally, this is your most special day ever, so **HAVE FUN!**

THE DIVA TRAVELLER

Having lived in sticky, hot Mumbai all my life, nothing says holiday more to me than being ankle-deep in snow, bundled up in thick woollies. Simply put, I'm a winter person. Take me to the mountains or anywhere cold and all my troubles just disappear. I know people who live in cold climates die for the sun, but I honestly love everything about winter. Waking up to fresh snowfall, going skiing down pristine white mountain slopes, sipping piping hot coffee in front of a fireplace and snuggling close to your man, you feel it's the most romantic season of the year. And everyone knows I'm a sucker for romance.

Thank God, Saif thinks exactly like me. Our favourite place to holiday, where we first went for his birthday after wrapping up the *Tashan* shoot, just happens to be one of the most beautiful places in the world. Every year, we make a trip to Gstaad, which is like a second home. As I've said before, we always stay at the Palace Hotel, where the staff now know us by name. Even the chef knows exactly what we like: grilled avocado and cheese sandwich with tons of fresh greens for me, and juicy grilled steaks for Saif. Our room also has a view of the mountains, and it's my holiday morning ritual to sit by the window with my cup of coffee and just spend a few minutes looking at the scenery.

One of the reasons we click so well as a couple is that we both love to travel. And we love surprising each other with impromptu holidays. When

we were shooting for *Qurbaan* in New York, I had fallen ill. But we couldn't stall the shoot, so despite being under the weather, I had to suck it all in and finish the job. Saif, being the thoughtful caring man that he is, planned a trip to Milan without my knowing a thing. It was such a fantastic surprise when he told me, because I really needed a break, but was too tired to plan one. We stayed at this gorgeous 16th-century villa at Lake Como, which felt like stepping back in time and landing in a fairytale. Saif also banned all work-related phone calls on that trip, so we really got a chance to relax, reconnect and just have fun without any work hassles, which is so important for a couple. Especially when both of you are working around the clock.

After that trip, we try and take a break every few months, just to get some much-needed alone time. Even if it's just a week in London or five days in Switzerland, we both feel completely refreshed and rejuvenated when we get back, ready to get down to business again.

Climate Control

Since we both love travelling, our trick is to try and get the most out of the weather. Landing up at your long-awaited holiday destination during the wrong season can totally kill the fun of any trip. So make sure you do your research before booking your tickets. We pick our destinations depending on Mumbai's crazy climate. And whenever it gets too hot in the city during the summer, we escape to the mountains or London where it doesn't feel like we're melting to bits since the weather is much cooler. The thrill of being able to pack sweaters and boots into your luggage just adds to the fun. When the rain and muck starts making life difficult in June, a trip to a beach town instantly brings the sunshine back into your life.

Planning in advance, rather than waiting for the last minute, also helps you get great deals on hotels and airline tickets. Scout multiple websites and compare prices to get the best offer. You never know, you could be staying at Claridges, one of London's most expensive hotels, for a steal if you just planned it right.

Packing Pointers

LUXE LUGGAGE

Experienced travellers will tell you bad luggage will really make your journey difficult. The last thing you want to be doing is trying to lug around a heavy suitcase with a broken handle. So invest in a good brand of suitcases, because those really can last a lifetime. I have some luggage from Louis Vuitton that have been all over the world, and have hardly even got a scratch. More reasonable options are available from Tommy Hilfiger, Samsonite and Longchamp. If you don't want to take a chance with someone else walking off with your bags, get luggage that can be easily identified. It's funny to see only black, blue and red suitcases on the luggage belt, and everyone craning their necks to try and see which one is theirs. And you should always have some sort of identification on your bag just in case it gets lost. Putting your name and the address of your hotel will really increase your chances of having your things returned.

SHOE BAGS

Suede and patent leather tend to get scuffed if you don't wrap them up carefully, and the heels might ruin your clothes. Shove little pouches of potpourri to keep them smelling fab! Put shoes in separate cloth bags and distribute them around your suitcase. That way, the weight evens out and you'll find it easier to carry the bags.

WATERPROOF VANITY

Get a waterproof bag for your make-up and bath products. I once dumped my sunscreen at the last minute into a corner of the suitcase, without taking care to seal the cap. It must have been a pretty bumpy ride, because by the time I opened my bags, the sunscreen was all over my shirts and dresses. And the oily stains were impossible to get rid of. Most of the five-star hotels have lovely products that you can count on instead of carrying your own, but if there's something specific that you use and don't want to go without, then learn from my mistake and seal the cap with some tape.

SUIT UP

Carrying formal jackets is always a problem, because you obviously don't want to fold them up and ruin them. I usually pack everything else first, and then just lay the jacket out on top. Another option is getting suitcases that have a special internal compartment for carrying jackets, but those can be a bit pricey.

MUST-PACK ITEMS: Basic over-the-counter medicines like motion-sickness and stomach-ache tablets, hair straightener or curling iron, phone charger with multiple socket options, emergency cash tucked into a corner of your suitcase.

Winter Wonderland

One of the best things about a holiday is that I finally get a chance to wear all my winter clothes. Boots, jackets, shawls, sweater dresses: I keep buying them when I'm travelling abroad and wait for a chance to wear them, which of course never happens in Mumbai. So packing is actually one of the most-fun parts of the trip. I get to have my own little mini fashion show, trying on different clothes and deciding on which to carry along. I think it takes more expertise to be fashionable in winter, because you can really get lost under all those layers. When it's about 5 degrees outside and your teeth are chattering from the cold, looking 'hot' means piling on as many sweaters as you can so that your brain doesn't go numb. You couldn't be bothered about how you look, because at that point, you're just trying not to freeze to death. Which is why you have to be prepared with all the right clothes and accessories, so that your fashion sense, unlike the temperature, won't hit zero.

Turn the page for The Art of Layering Up

The Art of Layering Up

The key to staying warm and stylish in the cold is layering. Don't forget that even when it's really freezing outside, all hotels and restaurants have internal heating. You won't want to be buried under layers of clothing at a fancy restaurant, or have to start an impromptu striptease for the guests.

- Start with a **THERMAL UNDERSHIRT**, and build your look from there. You could add a silk blouse, dinner jacket and knitted scarf and then throw on a heavy Burberry tweed jacket and gloves, for example, so you'll need to knock off only two layers once you're safely inside.

- Keep your legs toasty by wearing thermal socks inside knee-high suede or leather **BOOTS**, a look that's really stylish, but also really practical.

- Carry loads of **THICK WINTER SOCKS** in bright happy colours, which you can easily stuff into the corners of your suitcase and in between clothes. I wear them with my boots when I'm out or to bed when I'm ready to snuggle down under the covers. Thermal stockings are another option you could try if you're wearing a short dress and high-heeled pumps for the evening. If it's not too cold outside, I prefer wearing plain warm leggings and boots with a sexy sweater dress for an effortlessly chic look.

- Knitted **SWEATER DRESSES** are a good way to combine two layers into one. Look for one that hugs the body, and comes down to the knees for maximum protection. You can wear it with warm leggings tucked into boots to complete the ensemble.

- A **THICK LONG JACKET** will be your best friend in the winter, so spend some money on the best one you can afford. Montclaire makes the best snow jackets in the world, absolutely no argument there. I have a few from Burberry and Christian Dior too, and they just never seem to go out of style. I like the classic trench that comes down to my knees, though I also have a few short parkas that I wear to go skiing. When buying a

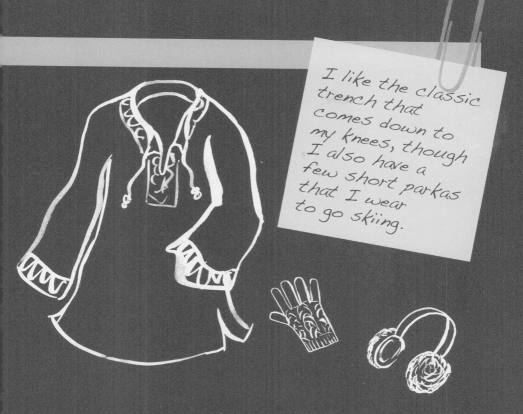

I like the classic trench that comes down to my knees, though I also have a few short parkas that I wear to go skiing.

jacket, try it on in the store , with a few layers underneath to see how it fits. It shouldn't be too tight around the arms and waist, or you won't be able to move comfortably when you're actually out in the cold.

- One winter accessory that I love is the **EAR MUFF**, the furrier the better. Your ears are especially sensitive to the cold, and leaving them exposed might actually make you fall ill. I have a fab pair of fluffy white ones from Burberry, which do a great job of blocking out the wind when I'm out on the ski slopes. And they're so cute and soft they actually put me in a good mood. You could also use a heavy scarf to protect your ears, but my vote is with the ear muffs.

- Ladies, remember that your hands and feet will get cold quicker than your body. Keep your hands nice and cosy by wearing **THICK GLOVES** whenever you're outside, especially if you're in the snow. I like leather gloves which fit well and don't have that synthetic feel. But gloves are available in a variety of options. Woollen ones in bright colours look pretty cute and you often get them with matching woollen caps.

- **SCARVES AND SHAWLS** are very important, not only because they can be worn with many different outfits, but also because they're easy to pack. Just stuff them into the corners of your suitcase or wherever there are a few extra gaps.

Get that Gorgeous Blush!

The winter also does wonders for my skin. Having a British grandmother means I'm genetically suited to the cold. Instead of my skin getting dry and chapped and starting to crack, it actually begins to glow and get rosy pink. So I don't even have to carry my make-up along, except for my Lakme kajal of course. But Indian skin doesn't always respond well to low temperatures, and you need to be prepared to keep skin problems away.

- Carry **TONS OF THICK CREAM** to keep your skin soft and supple. The cold sucks all the moisture out of your skin, leaving it prone to dryness. You might even start developing white patches on your face, hands and legs where the skin gets dry and stretched. Since creams for the body tend to be pretty thick, you might want to pack a lighter lotion for the face into your handbag, so you can use it whenever you feel your skin is getting too dehydrated. I love using Body Shop's scented body butter on my arms and legs, Emami cold cream and Clinique moisturiser on my face.

- Use a **MILD FACE WASH** because it also dries out the essential oils from your face. Clinique and Boots are trusted brands, or you could even go with a mild herbal face wash that won't irritate the skin.

- Use **SUNSCREEN** when you're out in the snow. I'm sure you're thinking, 'Huh? Sunscreen on the mountains?' Well, being high up means you're actually closer to the sun, and the snow tends to reflect a lot of light. So avoid those UV rays by slathering on some light Lancaster sunscreen. Or kill two birds with one stone and buy a moisturiser which has a good SPF value.

Beach Bum

I've been going to Goa ever since I was a kid, and it's still one of my favourite places to go to for a quick get-away. If I'm getting a bit tired of the city and need a recharge, I just hop onto a flight and spend the weekend on the beach or by the pool. And voila! Good as new. I'd say beaches, for me, are good for shorter holidays or if I'm heading out with a big gang. I celebrated my twenty-sixth birthday in Goa with a bunch of family and friends and it was a total blast. We were partying until early morning, lying around the pool all day and playing water games till we couldn't move. By the end of the trip, nobody wanted to leave, and we literally looked like we were being punished. Everybody came back with such crazy tans; it took weeks to return to normal. There's something about the beach that makes a holiday more laidback and carefree, which is the perfect way to spend catch up with old friends. Though, going for a midnight swim in a sexy swimsuit with your man is a pretty hot way to holiday too.

Tanned, Toned and Perfect!

The first time I wore a bikini on screen in *Tashan* was a nerve-wracking experience. First of all, the shoot was supposed to have happened in Pangong Lake in Ladakh in June, when the weather was bright and sunny. But we were not able to get the shot then, and the bikini, (or bikinis, since Aki brought three different colours, red, lime green and black, the final choice depending on where we were going to shoot) travelled around with us to Jaisalmer, and then down south. When they finally decided to shoot the bikini scene, we were in Greece in January, the height of winter. The water was minus 3 degrees, and the entire crew was wrapped up in boots, sweaters and jackets. Vaibhavi Merchant, the choreographer, needed to mark out the exact spot from where I would be rising out of the water, so she asked one of her assistants to stand in my spot. He was only knee-deep, but he was shivering with cold, so you can imagine how crazy it was for me to be submerged completely.

Even though my body was in the most bikini-ready shape of my life, there was so much preparation that went into making sure it looked great on screen, especially since it took almost nine months for us to actually get the shot. My yoga and diet had already given me flat abs, toned arms and slim thighs, but the camera picks up on every tiny detail. So for a shot that lasted just a few minutes, I had to go through waxing, full body scrubs and hours of make-up to get that beach goddess look. Luckily for you, it doesn't have to be that hard.

- A **TRIP TO THE SALON** a few days before your vacation is a must, especially if you're going to be baring it all in a swimsuit. Waxing those exposed areas means less time spent within the bathroom with a razor and more time on the beach, so that's something I would definitely recommend. If you have the guts and the pain threshold, go for a Brazilian body wax. It may hurt while you're getting it, but trust me, your clean look will be appreciated.

- Buy a good **WATERPROOF SUNSCREEN**. There's no point in covering yourself religiously with sunscreen only to have it all washed off when you hit the water. Most pharmacies stock sunscreens that aren't too harsh on the skin, so ask the person at the counter for their recommendation.

- Make sure you pack a **LARGE HAT** to protect your face from the sun, a beach cover-up for getting from the pool to your room, flip-flops so you don't ruin your pretty sandals in the sand, and an extra sling bag to pack a few essentials when you're ready to hit the beach.

Get the Right Swimsuit

For years, Indian women have been stuck with those super-ugly swimsuits with sleeves, high necks and attached frills, which do absolutely nothing for the figure. For some reason they remind me of the costumes worn by circus clowns. Yuck! Even if you can't imagine stepping out in a string bikini, there are a few other options which are fun and stylish, and won't make you blush.

The Bikini

I don't think you need to have a size-zero body to wear a bikini. Though I probably won't wear a two-piece on screen again, I still wear them when I'm holidaying in the Maldives. I think the bikini looks even better with my curves, and I know for a fact that Saif agrees with me. If you've decided to give the bikini a try, get the right style for your body type.

• If you're small-chested, you could get away with wearing a **STRAPLESS BANDEAU** top. But this is a strict 'avoid' for curvier girls as it offers your assets no support at all. • **HALTER-NECKS** with thicker straps look sexy and offer good support for bigger women. • If you're pear-shaped, go for **HOT SHORTS** or a **SWIM SKIRT** instead of bikini bottoms. They will make you feel less exposed, and give your butt a good shape. • A **STRING BIKINI** is something that is reserved for the bravest, and the skinniest of women. Ideally, nobody above a chest size 32 B should even consider it. There's a fine line between sexy and slutty, and the string bikini falls in the centre of no man's land.

The Tankini

A great option for covering up problem areas around the stomach and hips. The upper half feels like a regular tank top, and the shorts will protect your modesty if you're the sporty type who likes to play a game of volleyball on the beach. Most come with a built-in bra, offering extra support for top-heavy girls.

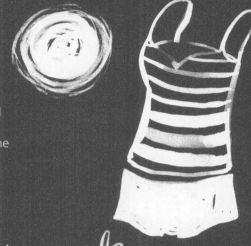

The Monokini

Just as sexy as a bikini, but it offers just a little more coverage on the stomach. You'll be surprised by how much of a mental difference that makes. Of course, you must be ready for a funny-looking tan if you spend too much time out in the sun.

The Classic One-piece

If you'd much rather step out in a regular swimsuit, have fun by getting one in a bright colour or print, or maybe even a one-shoulder version. You can even get creative with a plunging back or criss-cross straps. It's a good compromise between sexy and safe.

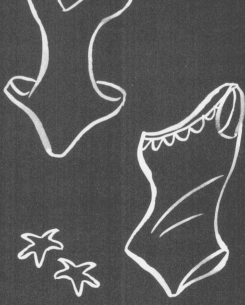

Swimsuit Brand Guide

Emilio Pucci makes very sexy printed bikinis, perfect for those women who have the bodies and want to flaunt them. I may not be a big fan of **Herve Leger**'s bandage dresses, but their swimsuits are great quality and last really long. **Victoria's Secret** and **Agent Provocateur** also have swimsuits for every shape, not just for those supermodels you see on magazine covers. If you're shopping on a budget, sportswear brands like **Adidas** and **Puma**, and high-street labels like **Mango** and **La Senza** offer wallet-friendly options that don't compromise on quality.

Summer Dressing

If you're headed to the beach for a holiday, the advantage is you'll be travelling light. **BRIGHTLY PRINTED COTTON DRESSES** and **SHORTS WITH GANJIS** in different colours should make up most of your wardrobe. Since you've already gone through the pain of a full wax job, take advantage of your smooth legs by showing them off in short skirts and hot shorts. Have fun with **PRINTS AND COLOURS**—the brighter the better—and don't be afraid to experiment. **KAFTANS** and light **OVER-SIZED SHIRTS** are perfect for using as a cover-up over your swimsuit. You can just throw it on when you're heading out of the room, and stuff it inside your beach bag once you get to the water. Brands like Roberto Cavalli make great beachy kaftans that are so stylish you can wear them to a pool party too.

If you're headed to a beach town, chances are you'll be doing plenty of partying. So don't forget to carry along a couple of sexy **COCKTAIL DRESSES** to wear when you dance the night away.

UNDERNEATH YOUR CLOTHES ...

I hated the thought of going to boarding school. Being far away from my family, friends and all the fun and excitement of Mumbai was a terrifying thought. So I did everything in my power to avoid going. I even tried failing the Welham Girls school entrance exam on purpose, just so that they wouldn't accept me. But my mother was even more stubborn than her mischievous daughter. She was determined to give me a healthy dose of discipline from the best institution in the country, even if she had to drag me there, kicking and screaming.

Going to a boarding school teaches you big lessons about life. Girls learn the importance of manners, obedience, books ... and the right undergarments. Anyone who's been to a girl's school will tell you this is the most important part of your uniform. Since you're all growing into women together, conversations about bras and panties are pretty common. You could learn from each other's experience, get advice on what brands are best, and the latest styles that your mom was probably not up-to-date about.

Boarding school also gave me a certain sense of conservatism when it came to lingerie. Even today, I'm

not the kind who can wear a sheer top with my bra showing through. In school, that would have got me punished before I could even blink. That's why one of my pet peeves is seeing a panty peeking out from the top of your jeans. You see a lot of very fashionable women hanging out in malls and stores wearing super-low-waist jeans. And the minute they bend over, they're either showing off their Calvin Klein thongs, or worse . . . you get a glimpse of their butt crack. It's just disgusting! There's a reason it's called underwear. It's not meant to be paraded, except in the bedroom.

BUYING THE RIGHT BRA

I am a Victoria's Secret girl. So, I cannot emphasise enough the importance of a good bra. Honestly, it's the bra that makes your boobs look good. Even women with small chests can create the illusion of curves with the right push-up. And ladies who are well endowed in this area need the right support, or the girls will look tired and droopy. And we all know that's not a good look on anyone.

I have a **3S RULE** for buying the right bra: **S**ize, **S**upport and **S**ex Appeal. See over the page.

Size

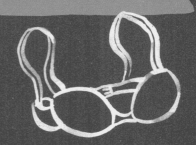

It's just ridiculous that many grown women who've been wearing a bra almost all their lives are completely clueless about their real size! Sure, we'd all like to be a classic 32C, but let's get real. We're curvy, sexy, voluptuous women and there's no shame in walking into a lingerie store and asking for a 34D, if that's what you really need.

Luckily, today, most stores have smart saleswomen who can help you find your perfect fit. And remember, the bust size changes every time you gain weight or lose a couple of kilos. I read once that women's bra sizes keep changing throughout their lives. When I was a Size Zero, obviously, I had lost weight on my torso and chest. So my bra size reduced. Once I gained few kilos, I had to get myself measured again so that I wouldn't be wearing a bra that was too tight to breathe in.

Get fitted every time you buy a new bra, especially if you're shopping for one after a few months. The perfect size should hug your torso firmly, without cutting into your back or riding up to your shoulders. The straps should hold everything in place nicely without needing major adjustments. Of course, there shouldn't be any extra fabric if it's a soft cup bra or extra space if the cups are moulded. If you're falling short of any of these requirements, then it's time to head back to the rack. Some brands, especially in India, don't stock certain sizes, and while I think that's blatant discrimination, don't fall for the 'cross-over' size story, unless you're really desperate. Most brands, whether you prefer the high-end La Perla or are happy with paisa-vasool Marks & Spencer, have different sizing charts, so the only way to really know if it's your size is to try it on.

Support

Like any good companion, your bra should offer you support in the most difficult situations. No point buying those extra-dainty balconette bras with slim straps if you're generously endowed in the chest area, and spend the rest of the day fidgeting uncomfortably. Different dresses also require different bras, depending on the fabric and neckline. Finding the right shape that offers unflinching support is the key to protecting your assets.

The best bra for your figure:

THE BALCONETTE Perfect for women with a small chest, this offers up enough cleavage to enhance your curves and looks great on a low neckline. A high-street brand that I've discovered for practical, yet pretty, balconette bras is Amante, available at almost all departmental stores.

THE PUSH-UP They're becoming increasingly popular, thanks to what Wonderbra did for their image, especially with those who'd like a little non-surgical help in the bust area. Again, this is best suited for smaller cup sizes, and could appear tacky on a healthier frame. You don't want to seem like you're spilling out of your top now, do you? La Senza and Triumph have budget-friendly options in a wide range of colours.

UNDERWIRE FULL CUP Made for voluptuous women, these come with soft or moulded cups, and hold it all in with no chance of spillage. The underwire adds to the support system, and gives you a great shape, and the best part is all brands stock this style in plenty.

THE T-SHIRT BRA Every woman needs a seamless T-shirt bra that won't show up under her favourite V-neck. In fact, I usually prefer to wear a fitted T-shirt when shopping for lingerie, just to make sure that I'm getting the best value for my money.

STRAPLESS This is where you should invest maximum energy and money, because a sturdy strapless bra will keep you happy and fidget-free through a night of dancing in your sexy one-shoulder top. Look for a version with a wide band and strong underwire support, no matter what size you are.

THE CORSET Yes, it's still around! Now a version of the strapless bra is the corset, which also has the additional advantage of sucking in your stomach. Usually available in skin tones, they are not the sexiest things in the world, but can offer your figure a helping hand, where exercise and dieting have failed. Spanx is a really popular brand abroad that makes suction-style underwear that you will swear by.

THE SPORTS BRA Fitness fashionistas, there's no leaving home without one in your gym bag. They should be made from sturdy fabric and hold everything in place when you hit the treadmill. I find the best ones are usually made by sportswear brands like Nike, Adidas and Lacoste, and not traditional lingerie labels.

THE NUDE BRA Lots of women have the same question: what kind of bra should I wear if my white blouse is slightly transparent? Thought the answer was white? Wrong! A white bra is only slightly better than wearing a black one, but the colour you're looking for is nude. Flesh-coloured bras create an even canvas under the shirt, so nothing is really highlighted. But this works only if you're wearing light pastel colours. Wearing a nude bra under a black top, especially if you have to face cameras like me, will only make it look like your boobs are popping through your top. And that photo will haunt you for life.

Sex Appeal

When you've taken care of the basics—size and support—you can indulge yourself a little in the sex appeal department. Personally, I love pretty pastel colours which can look both cute and sexy. And since lace is a fabric only women can wear, the combination of a lovely pastel-coloured lace bra is the epitome of feminine sensuality. Show me a lovely lavender balconette bra with lace straps and a delicate bow on the front, and I'm sold.

But don't be afraid to get really experimental if you're trying to spice things up in the bedroom. Indian women have the tendency to be shy and play it safe when it comes to lingerie shopping, but thank God that's changing now. Black leather corsets and animal prints can really drive your man wild, especially when he knows he's the only one invited to the show.

You can even buy some sheer negligees, if you can't handle the thought of wearing just a bra and thong to bed. The ones I like the most are like tiny baby doll dresses, that just about skim your thighs. They offer enough shelter for the body to give you confidence, while playing peekaboo. Seeing you half-exposed, half-covered up will really melt his brain, trust me.

Stockings, I have recently discovered, are a smart investment too when you're trying to figure out how to dress up a simple outfit. Patterned ones with hearts, zigzags or crisscross marks, available at high-street stores like Zara, Only, and Accessorize, can add quirkiness to a plain T-shirt and skirt combo. They're also known to cause an increase in heart rate when paired with stilettos and a garter, in the bedroom. You should give it a shot, but keep a pack of ice handy for when his jaw hits the floor.

Bottom Line

We've probably all had those days when we've decided to throw caution to the wind, pull on silky panties under our jeans, and spend the rest of the day squirming uncomfortably because it's just too hot. Putting on your sexy panties for no good reason is a thrill and a surprisingly good pick-me-up for when you're having a bad day. Just look how happy those Victoria's Secret models look all the time! But wearing the wrong type of underwear, now that can really ruin your day, especially when you're a busy working woman running around from one place to another. Panties need to comply with the three rules: feel comfortable, stay invisible, look pretty (but only when you're in your bathroom at home or with that special someone). Oh, and offer the right support. Seems funny to say it, but ill-fitting underwear can really change the shape of your derriere. I'm not going to treat my best asset with anything but the utmost respect and care, right.

BRAND GUIDE La Perla and **Victoria's Secret** undoubtedly make the best panties in the world. They're luxurious, yet comfortable, and have enough options in different styles to make your head spin . . . and his eyes pop. And who can forget Victoria Beckham's gorgeous ads for **Armani** lingerie. If it's good enough for Lady Beckham, it's definitely good enough for you. But if you don't want to take out a loan just to cover up your butt, **La Senza** and **Marks & Spencer** panties are pocket-friendly but still look stunning.

Pick the Right One

Here's a quick guide to buying the right type of panty to go with your wardrobe choice for the day.

THONGS I'll admit that wearing thongs aren't the most comfortable option for everyday wear, even if Sarah Jessica Parker insists she never leaves home without one. Lace thongs might be slightly more tolerable because the fabric is thin and won't irritate you. But thongs are a must-have to avoid that blasted panty line! Plus if you want to up that sexy quotient, nothing like a flimsy thong!

BOY SHORTS For a more practical, but still panty-line-proof version, I reach for my Victoria's Secret lace boy shorts or the seamless silk ones. Boy shorts are almost like men's briefs, hence the name. But they are the most comfortable things ever, and still manage to be sexy, especially if you buy them in lace or silk. For a cuter, preppy, everyday look try on the cotton ones that come in a million colours and designs!

BIKINI The bikini cut doesn't work for women with big hips and love handles. It will cut into your sides and create that ugly muffin shape that makes you look lumpy. But for those who are petit and toned this would be your ideal style.

MID RISE Mid-rise panties have the widest seat, so if you've got a bigger derriere, this is probably the right size for you.

LOW RISE If you're a fan of low-rise jeans, make sure you stock up on panties that are cut low in the back. Please don't be one of those tacky women who have their underwear peeking over the band of their jeans.

BRIEFS But for our tropical climate, it's best to put hygiene above everything else and stick to good ol' cotton panties.

CHOOSE THE CHOOS!

Once, in a magazine interview, I said the difference between shoe ladies and bag ladies is that shoe ladies are just a bit classier. Finished! That started World War III among all the women I knew. I only meant that shoes do more for your look and body than bags do! It's unarguable that the right shoes can really add elegance to an outfit, and to the person who's wearing them. Take a pair of high heels, for instance. Suddenly, you're looking taller, shoulders back, body curved. There's an extra sexiness to your movement, provided you're not tottering around in heels that are too high and uncomfortable, of course. You begin to walk with a grace and poise that will definitely get people to sit up and pay attention. Men may not notice what shoes you're wearing, but they'll certainly notice you in them. This I know for a fact.

Bags, on the other hand, are just arm candy to make other women jealous. All these limited edition Louis Vuittons and Birkins that we ladies go gaga over—no boyfriend ever notices the bag you're carrying and says, 'Oh sweetheart, that bag really makes you look gorgeous today.' You see what I mean?

That's not to say I don't get excited to see a gift-wrapped box with the Hermès logo and a card with my name on it. I'm just as much of a nut about buying new totes and sling bags as anybody else. But if I had to choose between the latest 'IT'

bag and a pair of Jimmy Choos, I would choose the Choos. Saif often jokes that if our apartment ever catches fire, before looking for him, I'd probably be trying to save my shoe collection. But he's one to talk! He treats his shoes like they're human, carefully cleaning them and wrapping them in paper before putting them in the closet. I, on the other hand, knock mine off at the door and forget about them.

My earliest memory of high-heel fascination is secretly trying on my mother's black patent leather pumps when I was a kid ... and nearly breaking my ankle. While I was busy modelling around in the Cinderella shoes, wearing a sari that I had converted into a ball gown, the heel got caught in the hemline, taking me down and leaving a giant tear in the Benarasi silk. My poor mother only discovered it much later when she was getting dressed to go to a wedding, and she just couldn't figure out how it happened. Sorry Mom!

Shoes were the one thing I collected obsessively, even when I was a teenager. Back then it was nothing fancy. I'd get just as excited about finding a really cool pair of chappals on Linking Road as I get today about my Galliano boots. You know it's true love when you don't care about where something came from or how much it cost. All that matters is that it's now yours.

FINDING YOUR SOULMATE

I'm not an extremist, except when it comes to shoes. I have this strange belief that they should either be really high, or flat. I remember trying on outfits with my stylist for an awards show recently, and I got so annoyed with the shoes I was wearing. Poor Tanya was trying to figure out whether they were too tight or not the right style. I had to tell her the problem: they just weren't high enough!

My name became linked to footwear, and everybody suddenly found out about my high-heel fetish during the shooting of *Kambakkht Ishq* in 2009. My stylist Aki Narula and his team went over and beyond, trying to get every pair of shoes they could get their hands on. I was super excited to go to 'Hair and Wardrobe' on the sets every day, just dying to see what they had picked out for that particular scene. I think there were more than fifty styles that were finally shown on screen, and I'm pretty sure they were the highest heels ever worn in a Bollywood film, that too for regular scenes. The shoes should seriously have appeared as junior artistes in the credits, because there were probably more shots of them in the movie than my own face!

That film also started the trend of wearing shoes and bags in contrasting colours. Aki would actually take care not to match the shoes to the dress, rather than the other way around. He put together such ridiculous combinations as a yellow dress with red shoes and a purple clutch, something I would never have done if it was up to me. But it worked, it looked stunning, and nobody could stop talking about it.

It's still one of my movies that people remember the most, all thanks to the wardrobe. Especially those shoes!

Heels

BLOCK HEELS

They are invariably in and out of fashion, but remain the comfier and easier heel to manage. I know a lot of women who couldn't be happier than when they're back in stores and in fashion. They can be super high, and still comfortable, because the bottom is so much wider than the stiletto and can support your weight better. Block heels also comes in many different shapes: there's a round version, that looks like an upside down ice cream cone, a straight version like the ones Marc Jacobs had on his runway a season ago, a curved one, like the shiny ones Prada just showed. The classic Mary Jane with a strap across the front looks really cute with block heels. If you're a boardroom babe with plenty of PowerPoint presentations and meetings to attend, these are the heels for you.

Sadly, even Superwoman won't last for more than a couple of hours in a pair of stilettos

STILETTOS

Those thin, pointy heels that are so gorgeous and so painful all at the same time. They're definitely the sexiest kind of heel, not only for the way they look, but for the way they make you look. Your body arches out, your bum looks higher and perkier and your calves look long and toned. But sadly, even Superwoman won't last for more than a couple of hours in a pair of stilettos. It's one of the downsides of being a movie star: standing for photographs on the red carpet and then posing for hours in super-high heels. By the end of the night, after four hours of standing, my feet go numb. Then all I can dream of is collapsing on my nice soft bed.

WEDGES

Another creation of comfort is the wedge heel. I don't own too many myself, because I feel it makes my ankles look slightly thicker, but they are very comfortable, especially for women who aren't too confident of walking in heels. The entire base of the shoe has continuous support in terms of a heel which distributes your weight evenly, and you won't even realize you've become four inches taller.

PLATFORMS

They were a rage in the '70s, and they've come back with a bang, in a chic, modern form, of course. Some heels that look shockingly high are actually a lot more comfortable than you think because the front is also raised with a supporting platform. But this is the kind of shoe that needs to fit you perfectly. If it's too loose and you trip, you're guaranteed a sprained ankle.

MATCH YOUR STYLE

KITTEN HEELS The most practical heel you can have in your closet is a pair of sturdy round-toe pumps with a 3-inch heel. They're the mammas of the shoe world: supportive, familiar and not too flashy. You can wear them to any occasion—party, boardroom meeting, PTA conference, dinner—and they won't stick out oddly. Personally, they're not the kind of shoes I'd jump at, but everybody needs a pair of sensible heels. Even me. **Pair them with** pencil skirts, formal dresses, summer dresses and maybe even that pant-suit.

POINTY-TOED PUMPS I'm not too sure about these. They just seem like weapons instead of shoes, especially the ones that stick out about three inches in front on you. I can imagine going out dancing at a club and stabbing everyone around me in the ankle by mistake. Yikes! **Pair them with** short or knee-length skirts, or skinny trousers. I prefer to avoid them when wearing long gowns that cover the entire leg, because then they make my feet seem heavy and clunky.

PEEP-TOES My absolute favourite. They're super cute and have the grip of a pair of pumps, without being completely closed. They also make your feet look dainty and delicate, so that's always a plus point. I have them in all the possible colours, including electric blue and parrot green because they just go with everything. Louboutin makes some gorgeous peep-toe shoes, and you could wear red nail paint to match the bright red soles. **Pair them with** your entire wardrobe. You can wear them with long skirts or gowns, because the little glimpse of your toes balances out the fact that your legs are completely covered. They don't make you look shor and stubby like a pair of round pumps might. They even work with jeans and shorts, because they could look cool and casual, unlike closed shoes.

STRAPPY HEELS Look great on delicate slim feet that have recently been treated to a pedicure. I can't stand seeing a lovely pair of heels, and then see dirty, cracked feet sticking out of them. My single most beloved style is my Yves Saint Laurent Tribute heels, the T-strap platform sandals. They have the best grip, and even though they're super tall, I never feel like I'm going to slip and fall. I have them in every colour, and Karisma and I keep hoping that they'll expand the collection so we can buy even more. If you have wider feet, opt for thicker straps which won't cut into your skin. Grip is very important when wearing strappy shoes because if your foot slips, you could really be in a lot of pain. **Pair them with** more casual clothes, like short dresses or jeans. They can also look elegant under a red-carpet gown, provided they've got some bling on them, and your nails are bright and polished. I also like wearing them with saris, something you shouldn't do with closed pumps, please.

My single most beloved style is my Yves Saint Laurent Tribute heels, the T-strap platform sandals.

Flats

As much as I love heels, obviously I can't wear them night and day. The day is reserved for flats, unless I have an event to go to. And when I'm just lounging around the house, or heading over to my mom's house for some tea and gossip, I'm usually in chappals. But by chappals, I don't mean bathroom slippers. I just hate those, even in the house. I'm talking about colourful Kolhapuris, thong slip-ons, platform chappals or lightweight ones with funky prints on the straps and soles.But flip-flops can actually drag your whole outfit down, if you're not careful, when you're walking. Chappals tend to make you shuffle like an old lady, and that 'krrrch krrch' sound of women dragging their feet really drives me up the wall. Though, in India where the weather can get as hot as it does, and the roads are as bumpy and pot-holed as they are, it can be very tempting to slip into flats for everything.

Flats

PLATFORM CHAPPALS I have to confess I actually own a couple of platform chappals with glittery straps! They may not be the most chic things to wear, but they are so, so comfortable that you have to drag them off my feet to get me to take them off. These are best worn at home!

STRAPPY SANDALS If you want to look a little better without trying too hard, choose a nice pair of strappy sandals instead. They're open enough to let your feet breathe, and won't make you look like you just rolled out of bed and out on to the street. These give a lovely summery look and are great with dresses and casual wear.

KOLHAPURIS Great with both ethnic and western wear. The best part is that you can play with colour on this one. It immediately gives a whimsical air to any outfit! And is that dash of street-wear you can happily add to your wardrobe.

GLADIATORS To feel a bit Greco-Roman, strap up! They're a little bulkier than your average strappy sandals, but can set off a dress or skirt ensemble and give it that laid-back dressy feel. These also look great with hot shorts. A nice tawny colour does the trick.

SNEAKERS I have a select few sneakers that I wear when working out and catching a flight. There's a new trend started of people really dressing up to catch flights, wearing jeans and high heels. Please, I can't be stuck in tight clothes and high heels on 16-hour flights, and have my legs swell up by the time I reach my final destination. All for the sake of a few photos. It also saves space in your baggage to wear sneakers on the flight, since they're heavier and bulkier than your other shoes. Sneakers are useful and usually last long, so it's OK to splurge a little on getting a good pair from a top brand. Puma makes the most stylish pairs, and in fashionable colours too, while Nike, Adidas and Reebok are all known for their rock-solid pairs. I have a pair of sneakers that I bought almost a decade ago which still have a few good years left in them.

Boots

If you live in Mumbai like me, the tropical climate means you'll almost never get a chance to wear boots. So though I love, love, love this particular style, mine get a breath of fresh air only when I'm travelling. Slouchy boots one size bigger than your actual measurement are great for flights when you want to keep your toes warm without strangling them. Make sure you have enough room to wiggle around in, or you might have to surgically detach them from your feet after a few hours.

The best thing about boots is that the styles don't really change that much with different seasons, so you can invest in a really good pair and be sure to get your money's worth. I have a studded Yves Saint Laurent pair that look even better now that they're slightly scuffed and worn in. After all, those boots were made for walking.

BALLERINAS AND OXFORDS Personally, I don't really like wearing closed shoes, but ballet flats and oxfords look really cool on some people. I guess you could compromise if you're having a bad foot day by covering them up in a pair of girlie ballerina flats. Nobody will know the difference. Ballet flats are also beyond seasons, so don't worry about paying a little more for a decent pair. Steve Madden has some pretty pairs, and Zara always has a good collection which are very affordable. Even small boutique stores selling stuff from Bangkok in Bandra and Andheri have a whole bunch of ballet flats. Wear them with skinny jeans, a pleated skirt or even a pair of tailored shorts; they can pass almost any fashion test.

SHOES, BAGS AND MORE...

Bags

This is definitely a girl thing. I see men walking out of the house with both hands free, and all that they need stuffed into their trouser pockets. But tell a girl that she needs to leave her bag behind, and she'll look at you like you said they've banned Diwali. Our handbag is our faithful companion through the day. It becomes a carry-all, accessory, conversation starter, pillow ... even weapon when needed. And the funny thing is, I'm not really sure what we put in there, because I've realized that no matter how big the bag is, we always manage to fill it.

Bag Your Bag

If you need help deciding what bag to invest in, I'm happy to help.

THE TOTE When God created woman, I think his first words were, 'Here's your tote. You'll thank me for it one day.' I do not know a single woman, young or old, who doesn't own one. It's the biggest of the handbag family, and is usually made of soft material so it can change shape to suit your purposes. It needs to have sturdy straps to balance the weight, and have multiple pockets inside to store your make-up, purse, cell phone, keys, and any other kick-knacks that tend to get lost easily. Prada bags are my current obsession, though I've gone through the Hermès and Louis Vuitton phase too.

THE SLING These have become very popular because they leave the arms free and stay close to the body so you know your stuff is safe. The strap should be easy to adjust, and strong enough not to snap if you decide to jam-pack the bag. The slightly larger version of the sling is the messenger bag, though these have a slightly masculine look to them. Chanel's quilted sling bag is everybody's ultimate obsession, but all high-street brands from Nine West to Aldo also stock funky options.

THE CLUTCH How would we ever go to a party without a fits-in-your-palm bag that stocks all our essentials? Alexander McQueen's clutches are legendary, especially the ones with the little knuckle-duster clasp on top. They're the perfect match of beautiful and badass. Judith Leiber's bejewelled minaudières, which are so tiny that they're totally impractical but still utterly irresistible, are super popular with celebrities; and Indian designer Suneet Verma has also designed a line for them with Indian influences.

The Style Diary of a Bollywood Diva 203

Sunglasses

Everyone knows the celebrity's favourite accessory is a pair of sunglasses. How could we deal with the non-stop flashes of the paparazzi cameras otherwise? There's an unwritten rule in the kingdom of Bollywood: the bigger the sunglasses, the bigger the star. The fact that they're also great for shielding the delicate undereye skin from the sun's damaging rays is totally secondary. But picking the right frames for your face can be tricky.

According to me, classic aviators with a chrome finish suit almost every face shape. The originals are from RayBan, but you get imitations in different styles from almost every eyewear brand now. Wayfarers are another flattering style that suits almost any face shape, so they even make great gifts. Audrey Hepburn made them famous in *Breakfast at Tiffany's*, and now every Hollywood celebrity worth a single photo has at least three pairs. You even get them in funky colours, so you can change up your styles every day.

For a more retro look, which many of the big fashion houses are now looking towards, think of big, round frames like Jackie Kennedy used to wear, or the classic cat's eye shape that they now make in different colours. Prada has super-fun sunglasses that I just love every season, but if you're not going to break the bank for eyegear, don't worry. All the high-street brands like Aldo, Fastrack, Accessorise and Mango also have sunglasses that are usually styles after the trend you see on the ramp.

Wayfarers are a flattering style that suits almost any face shape, so they even make great gifts. Audrey Hepburn made them famous

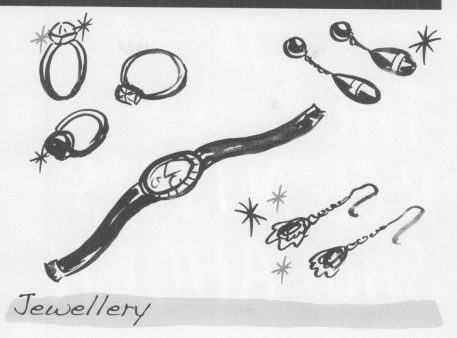

Jewellery

I've mentioned a hundred times how I'm not a big fan of jewellery. Only recently has Tanya turned me into a convert for statement neckpieces, but even that's only for the red carpet. I can honestly walk right by a jewellery store and not even feel a little tempted to peek in. Though, I love solitaires—as Saif will tell you! I don't really buy myself any bling but I love my little diamond handed over in a gift box.

I've always been more of a watch girl. I think a single classic timepiece on the hand can actually look as good as a gold bracelet. Many of them even come decorated with diamonds too. And God knows a watch from a top brand like Audemars Pigeut or Breguet will cost as much as the most expensive jewellery. I usually wear one non-stop till I get gifted the next one, and then I'll find excuses to wear that all the time. If you're looking for something that's beautiful and practical, invest in a super glamorous watch that will also last a lifetime and can be passed on to your daughter and grand-daughter as a vintage heirloom.

When it comes to earrings, I prefer simple solitaires for daily use. If I'm dressing up, then it's a toss-up between elegant drop earrings for western garments, and more opulent chandelier earrings for my saris. Somehow, Indian outfits look incomplete without a little jewellery, so this is one place where I make an exception to my rule.

THE RELENTLESS SHOPAHOLIC

'My name is Kareena Kapoor and I'm a Shopaholic.' I'm absolutely obsessed with retail therapy. If I'm not shopping when I'm on holiday, I'm online checking out the latest styles on Net-A-Porter.

My stylist Tanya tries to save me from my addiction. She keeps saying, 'But you already have this dress.' What she doesn't understand is this one's a different colour! I often land up buying more than one piece of the same thing, especially when it comes to shoes. My friends tease us saying that Lolo and I have bought so many versions of the Yves Saint Laurent Tribute heels that it's high time the company name the style after us. 'Yves-Saint-Laurent-Tribute-to-the Kapoor-Sisters-heels'. I have to say, the name does sound catchy.

And still, if I see a new colour in one of their stores when I'm abroad, I have to pick it up. I may actually love shopping even more than pizza. And everybody knows I would kill for pizza.

The only problem with this actress-shopaholic combination is that I just can't go out in my own city. First of all, I'd have photographers following me everywhere taking pictures. I'd have to be so careful about everything it would ruin all the fun. If I decide to go to

check out the new couture collection at Rohit Bal's store at the Palladium, the next day all the newspapers will have the same headline: 'Kareena parts ways with Manish Malhotra camp'. And can you imagine what would happen if they heard a pair of jeans didn't fit and I had to get one size larger? 'Kareena puts on weight—is she pregnant?' It's such a nightmare even to think about that I'd much rather hop on a plane to London and do my shopping there.

Though, I didn't always have this problem. I remember going chappal-shopping with my friends on Linking Road in Bandra. I knew all the unknown spots with the best deals, and we'd bargain like our pocket money depended on it. Back then, I actually thought Rs 300 for a pair of shoes was too expensive. We'd go through the whole process: walk away after the shop boy quoted his price, saying it was too much, they'd call us back, we'd all argue some more and finally, like all fights between men and women, we'd win. Imagine doing that at Gucci.

I still love street shopping, but I can only do it when I'm far away from home. When we were shooting in London for *Agent Vinod*, my team decided to check out China Town. Those are the best areas in any city to get good quality leather bags and jackets for really cheap. Since I love Chinese food, I decided to go with them. Roaming the streets was so much fun because nobody knew who I was. I could actually walk into any store and eat food from street stalls without worrying about starting a riot.

I always carry an empty suitcase when I'm travelling, because I know I'm going to come back with at least double the stuff. The only not-so-fun part is seeing the credit card bill. Every woman has had that month at least once in her life (OK, in my case, it maybe more than once) when the bill arrives and boom! You're hit by a tsunami of zeros. Suddenly, you realize that those canary yellow Jimmy Choo heels you thought you wouldn't be able to live without cost as much as a small car. I'm just glad Wikileaks doesn't hack into my credit card account, or my mom will march over to my house to give me a piece of her mind.

But what's the point in working hard for your money and not really enjoying it while you can? One of my favourite designers, the man with the red sole, Christian Louboutin, has a philosophy, 'Having more opportunities,' (he means money) 'means being able to experience more things.' And if I want to experience the pure thrill of wearing one of Mr Louboutin's $1,500 glitter pumps and feeling like a queen, that's not so wrong, is it?

Best Stores in India

Mumbai and Delhi

If I could hide behind sunglasses and a cap, or turn invisible, I would be able to visit these stores that I love.

MUMBAI

Manish is on my speed dial and I usually get first choice of everything he designs, but it's still fun to walk into his store and check out the gorgeous clothes arranged so beautifully. He's a one-stop-shop for all kinds of occasion, whether you have to go to a mehendi ceremony or a red-carpet party. **The Palladium** at High Street Phoenix has most of the top brands in one place, and it's probably one of the few places I can shop at in peace if I dash in and out without creating a fuss. They have a huge **Zara** store, which I inaugurated, and there's also **Diesel**, **DKNY**, **Emporio Armani** and **The Collective**, which stocks Diane Von Furstenberg and Vivienne Westwood. Jimmy Choo, Miss Sixty and Steve Madden are also under the same roof, so it's a mini shoe-shoppers'

paradise. **Aza** and **Kimaya** in Juhu are two multi-designer stores that have haute-off-the-ramp Indian designs for different tastes. **Ensemble** was one of the first designer stores, and they have big names like Tarun Tahiliani, Anamika Khanna, Savio Jon and Shahab Durazi as part of their store.

DELHI

Everybody tells me **Hauz Khas Village** is the new cool shopping destination in the capital, and after visiting the **Ritu Kumar** store there, I have to agree. It reminds me of The Grove in LA, full of hip little stores, cafes and designer boutiques, and some of the best dressed people I've seen anywhere. If I could go shopping to a mall, it would be **DLF Emporio** in Vasant Vihar. It's one of the few Indian malls that can compare to the ones abroad, and they have all the designer flagship stores under one roof, including my must-visit Christian Louboutin.

Shopping Abroad

London

A shopper's paradise. The British have a very quirky, cool sense of style. And they also have all the biggest brands, from high-street stores to super-expensive designer boutiques. I can spend days on **Bond Street**, taking breaks only to eat. **Harrods** is my favourite pit stop there, because they have all the best brands under one roof. I've realized that department stores often have the best collection of clothes, because they pick and choose what they know their customers will love from the designers' lines. That always makes the job easier for us shoppers. The last time I was there, I discovered **Paige**, a cool new brand of denims that fits my shape really well. I probably would never have heard of it if the salespeople hadn't decided it was worth stocking in their store. **Selfridges** is also fantastic, and my entire collection of boots is almost entirely sourced from within that department store.

And I never miss a chance to check out **Topshop**. It's the coolest high-street brand, and their store is so massive you can get lost inside. I pick up tons of basic T-shirts, ganjis and shorts there because the style is always so trendy. They also have lovely bags and shoes, which are not too expensive, for daily wear. I love that they tie up with big designers like Jonathan Saunders and Mary Katrantzou every few months, to make collections that are more affordable. Of course, people wait outside the store for hours to get in, and the entire line gets sold out within a few hours. Inside, people are pushing and shoving each other, racing around the store trying to get their hands on everything they can find. It's like training for the marathon.

While London has literally all the big brands, it also has beautiful boutiques run by very interesting young fashionistas. A small-store discovery I made there was **Sweaty Betty's**, where I pick up all my track suits from. It's such a fun store that I can get lost for hours there.

New York City and LA

I like going to the **Meatpacking District** when I'm in New York, because the designer stores there are like works of art. They're all so well-designed and beautifully laid out, that you don't really have to buy anything to feel satisfied. Can you believe that area was once full of just butchers' shops?

In Los Angeles, **Rodeo Drive** and **Robertson Boulevard** are on everybody's map. They have all the top brands in one line, from **Louis Vuitton** and **Fendi** to **Giorgio Armani** and **Prada**. I never forget to visit the **Ralph Lauren** store, because I love their simple chic clothing, especially the shirts. **Anthropologie** at The Grove is another store that stocks beautiful organic clothing from all over the world.

Paris

The most chic city in the world, and their stores are obviously very luxurious and very chic. Almost all the top designers have their stores here, and you can walk around **Avenue Montaigne** near the Champs-Élysées and find couture brands like **Dior** and **Chanel**. It's almost impossible to window-shop here, because the collections are so beautiful that you have to go inside to check them out more closely. Paris also has lovely little boutique stores tucked away in small corners that you'll never find unless you're on foot. When Saif and I are on holiday, we do a lot of walking around. It's the best way to discover a city; plus, it's good exercise.

Paris has a lot of vintage stores, which are lots of fun just to check out because we don't have that concept in India. You can find clothes and accessories from as far back as the '20s and '30s, mostly in very good condition. You might even find an original designer skirt or dress, which is like having a piece of history in your cupboard.

Dubai

The Middle-East, especially Dubai, is another place renowned for having some of the best shopping in the world. It's also just a couple of hours away, almost like going to Delhi, so you can even go just for the weekend. The top venues—**Mall of the Emirates**, **Dubai Mall**, **Burjuman Centre** and the **Ibn Battuta**—are like mazes, except that you will happily get lost inside. They also have a fab shopping festival in winter, where all the shops go on sale and people fly in from all over the world just to shop. The crazy discounts will make you lose your mind. Honestly, a shopaholic like me shouldn't be allowed to go anywhere near Dubai, but I can't help myself. The collections are always brand new, and the exchange rate isn't too high, so it fits almost all budgets. Just be careful not to start complaining about anything in Hindi, because it's very likely the salesperson in the store will understand you.

Bangkok

Not big on my radar as a holiday destination, but most people love heading there just to pick up a year's supply of clothing and shoes. My foot size is very small—36—so I actually find it very easy to get the right fit in this part of the world. The malls aren't really high-end though, and they even have some shopping centres which only sell wholesale. But if you're lucky, you might be able to convince them to sell you a single item for a decent price.

Shop Smart on Your Holiday

If, like me, you mostly shop abroad, sync your holiday to the **SALE SEASON**. Winterwear in Europe and the US goes on sale around April–May, summer collections around October–November. I find that sales in larger chain stores last longer while boutiques tend to have limited offers.

This sounds bizarre but I make a **TIMETABLE** to shop, so that I don't waste too much time inside stores. Two hours in Selfridges, one hour at Topshop … It helps you cover a lot of ground, especially when you don't have weeks to blow up doing nothing but shopping!

If you don't have too much time to shop—and this happens when you're with your husband or boyfriend!—**ORDER ONLINE** and get the stuff delivered to your hotel. Plan for a ten-day delivery period, at least, and inform your hotel so that they don't return the stuff thinking it's a mistake. Tell them it's a life-or-death situation and they'll understand. Your man will be so thankful that you didn't drag him to a hundred stores—he won't mind when the bill comes. Trust me!

Surf travel blogs and local websites to locate lovely little stores that you may miss otherwise. If I'm travelling to a new place, I always ask friends for recommendations. Just tweet it or upload it as your Facebook status … You'll have a deluge of suggestions on where to shop and what to avoid.

Plan your plastic: paper ratio smartly, depending on where you like to shop. Vintage stores, flea markets and street stalls tend to accept only cash while you can just swipe your card in malls or designer stores. The last thing you want is to fall in love with something and then realize they only **TAKE CASH**, which you didn't carry enough of! It happened to me. I had to buy three Hermès bags to cheer myself up.

If you have a **LOCAL FRIEND**, take him or her along. With someone to bargain in the local language, especially in touristy places, you can avoid being fleeced. You can always bribe them to come along with a pretty necklace or a pair of shoes—the bargains they manage will make it worth it!

PACK ULTRA-LIGHT when starting your holiday. I think my suitcases are jinxed though, because even when I barely shop, my bags are always overweight. It's black magic!

Online Shopping

If you can't go to the store, bring the store to you. Online shopping is God's gift to people who are too busy or too far away to get a great deal. I discovered it a few years ago when a friend recommended Net-A-Porter. That website is absolutely perfect. I thought it would be complicated to figure out but it was the simplest thing ever. It has tonnes of beautiful clothes, bags, and shoes from all kinds of brands from all over the world. It was love at first sight. Then someone suggested ASOS. Trendy clothes at high-street prices? Sign me up! It's among the few sites that used to deliver to India for free though now there are many more companies that have realized they should. I'd like to think my crazy shopping helped convince them.

Yes, I was suspicious about buying clothes without trying them on first. Would the Stella McCartney top I bought be the right size? What if it doesn't look exactly like it does in the picture? What if it's torn at the back and I only find out when they deliver it?

Finally, my adventurous side took over. I consulted friends who were already e-shoppers, took their advice on trustworthy websites, read all the fine print carefully ... And well, my Ralph Lauren silk shirt turned out to be exactly what I saw and expected. Really, it was just a five-minute job. Now imagine the time I'd have spent in taking a shower, getting dressed, getting into a car, then fighting traffic to reach a store ... In that time, by moving just my finger, I could literally possess a whole new winter wardrobe!

Ordering something online is like Christmas. Not only do I avoid paying all the extra taxes to buy designer clothes in India (those really make the clothes completely overpriced) but I come home to see beautiful packages, all gift-wrapped for me ... Ah, heaven!

Now, I'm such a pro that my mom and sister have turned me into their personal shopper. My friends take my advice on which sites offer the widest variety. What's more, now I can buy gifts online, instead of having to head out to the shops or getting someone else to buy them for me. And they get delivered to the doorstep, which is great to surprise someone who lives halfway across the world.

The one thing I will not buy online? Jeans. Those you have try on, even if you've worn the brand for years, because every style has a different fit. Oh, and boots. Flats or chappals are fine but it's safer to buy closed shoes like boots after you've tried them on and walked about in them. You don't want to hobble if the heel starts to wobble!

Online Shopping Tips

- First-time e-shopper? **ASK YOUR FRIENDS** for suggestions. The Internet is the world's biggest tourist spot, and it's easy to get sucked into a bad deal. If a website is highly recommended, then you're probably going to get good service.
- Read the site's **RETURN POLICY** carefully. Recently, I had a bad experience when a Valentino gown that I ordered was too big and had to be returned. The whole process took so long that it sucked all the fun out of ordering the dress. All online stores claim to make exchanges or give refunds. What you won't expect, though, is to pay the shipping charges for exchanges, and those can be quite steep! It also takes very long for them to reverse the charged amount

on your card, so don't panic if it isn't immediate.
- Different websites have different **SIZING** charts, and the clothes they offer can have dual sizing. Measure yourself regularly and cross-check with the sizes available online. Body-con dresses and tailored outfits tend to be unforgiving—a few extra inches and you might have to return your contour-caressing Fendi!
- Look for **DISCOUNTS** and deals. There's always some promotion or the other going on, and you might actually get a really good deal if you search.
- Many websites don't deliver free to India. Some don't ship to India at all. Check out their **DELIVERY** areas before you make up your mind to buy something.

TOP ONLINE STORES • Net-a-porter • Shopbop • Asos • Bergdorf Goodman • The Outnet • Yoox • Pret-Amoda

NEVER SAY BLONDE

Looking back at old photos can make or break your ego! Some people love pictures of when they had flawless skin and skinny bodies and could wear anything under the sun. But most people look back and shriek at their bad hair, terrible make-up, ghastly clothes ... 'How did I ever think this was cool?!' Permed hair with blonde highlights, extra-baggy jeans with torn tees ... Get my drift? Now imagine what happens when the WWW has thousands of photos of you! Thanks to Facebook and Twitter, you don't need to be a celebrity to know what I mean. There's no escaping my days as a blonde or that one time I had a really bad hair day but had to attend a premiere anyway.

In the film industry, you'd better make sure you're always camera ready or you have a good sense of humour. I chose the latter. I'm just not one of those girls who can wear high heels and immaculate make-up on a long-haul flight just for the shutterbugs at the airport. I'm human, and I will not look perfect all the time.

What we forget when we see a bad photo is how much fun we were having in that moment. Sure, you have your mouth wide open in that shot but that's because you were laughing so hard at a joke that you didn't have the time to pose. My mom had a rule: 'Take as long as you want in front of the mirror at home but once you leave, forget what you look like and just have fun!' That's a great tip, no matter what your age or profession. Dazzle them with your smile, floor them with your personality—they won't notice that your hair looks like you ran through a storm to get there.

I love experimenting with my roles. It's such fun playing completely contrasting characters from a bold, brash prostitute in *Chameli* to an impulsive college girl in *Jab We Met* to a simple teacher in *Kurbaan*. I work very hard to be believable. I mix up my wardrobe, trying out different silhouettes with my stylists. But the one thing I refuse to experiment with is my hair. Which is ironic, because I played a hairstylist in *Ek Main Aur Ekk Tu!* I think that was Karan's private joke because he knows how fussy I am. Even in the movie, my pink streak was a clip-on extension—I just couldn't allow them to come near my hair with a bowl of bleach. Call me boring but you'll never see me with bright green streaks or a super-short bob. I love my hair too much to do anything crazy to it.

Hair can make or break any look. You may have your clothes, accessories and make-up right but if you mess up your hair, there's no saving you! And that smile, it won't last all the way! So if you want to be a diva, mind your mane!

TRICK!

- **NO VOLUME?** Flip your hair upside down and blow-dry it from the roots up. Combine this with a volumizing shampoo and you'll be cheating your way to model-like hair!
- If your hair is **BRITTLE** and tends to break or split, be careful when brushing. Don't tug at the tresses, all at once. Separate it into segments and gently unravel all the knots with a wide-toothed comb. You can even use some serum to manage those little flyaways.
- **STRAIGHT** hair can often fall flat, especially if you live in a hot and humid climate, like I do. Work some styling mousse into your hair as you dry it to give it lift. Use a paddle brush to bring out the real shine. Every now and then, try air-drying for a wavy effect.
- **FINE AND LIMP** hair also tends to get greasy very quickly. If there's no time to wash it, quickly apply some gel for the wet, slicked-back look. You can also pull it up into a high knot or braid. But do not go to sleep with gel in your hair!
- **CURLY** hair is actually a gift, if you know how to style it well. Never use a comb on dry hair. While it's still wet, work in a little leave-in conditioner and comb gently with a wide-toothed comb. Out with the tangles, in with those gorgeous curls!

Perfect Cut!

Different face shapes deserve tailor-made haircuts. Follow my style sheet to see which look will work best on you.

SQUARE If you have a square-shaped face, like me, with a prominent jawline, avoid very short hair as it will only give you a very harsh boxy look. Let the hair start below the shoulder, with the first layer beginning at your jaw. This will help frame your face perfectly.

ROUND If your problem is puffy cheeks, an oval-shaped haircut will magically slim down your face. Let the first flick fall in line with your cheekbones. But definitely avoid cutting a fringe. You don't want to look like your cheeks are trying to take over your entire face! Side bangs could work, but they're very high maintenance and tend to get in your eyes a lot which can be quite irritating. If you're a working woman with not too much time to spend on styling, this is too fussy a chop.

OVAL Women with this shape are the luckiest, and can sport almost any hairstyle without too much of a problem. They can even try a choppy bob like the one Victoria Beckham made famous, or go even shorter if they have delicate features. But remember, there's a difference between a short haircut for a woman and a man's crop. My hairstylist, Pompy Hans, gets terribly upset when he sees women who look like the barber cut off all their hair in a fit of rage. The idea is to get enough texture and length in the right spots—think Princess Diana's elegant shag—so no one mistakes you for a particularly curvy boy from behind.

TRICK! The perfect hairstyle, which suits almost all face shapes and textures, is a mid-length cut with layers. Depending on the cut, layers can add volume to flat hair and bring extra-big curls under control. It's also the easiest to maintain, because you can pull it up into a ponytail or bun when you have no time to style it.

My Top Looks

Since my hair texture is fine and silky, without too much volume, Mumbai weather is really its biggest enemy. The heat, dust and humidity can turn me into a greasy mess in minutes, no matter how long I've spent in front of the mirror perfecting my do for the night. And imagine standing under hot studio lights for hours on top of all that. With the odds stacked against me, my hair doesn't really stand a chance. But you have to work with what you got! So figure out your hair and learn to work with it.

The Bouncy Blow-Dry

That's why my all-time favourite hairstyle is a no-fuss bouncy blow-dry. Think silky smooth hair that flows into gentle old-Hollywood waves. It's the most naturally glamorous style out there and usually suits most face shapes. It also makes the hair look glossier, because straighter hair reflects light better.

Pompy Hans, who's been my mane maestro ever since *Kambakkht Ishq*, knows this look is exactly what gets me excited about a red-carpet appearance. He's very talented, but I'm probably his most boring client because I don't allow him to try anything that's too elaborate or over-the-top. He knows that I'm not going to be able to sit still in the make-up chair for more than half an hour tops, so anything he tries needs to be quick and bang on.

I've learnt to do a blow-dry myself, for when I'm travelling or heading out to a private party. With the right tools—round brush, powerful dryer with a nozzle—and a bit of practice, it doesn't take me more than 20 minutes to go from girlie to glam. This look is also super versatile. It goes with gowns, jeans, saris and even a power suit, and it never looks like you just walked out of some costume party. Oh, and the effect it has on men? I promise, he won't be able to take his eyes off you when you walk into the room.

TRICK! If you're not a genius with the brush and blow-dryer like Pompy is, but you still want to get those gorgeous big waves at the tips, this is an easy way to get a similar look: begin with blow-drying your hair straight. When you're about 90 per cent done, work a little styling mousse through the length of your hair, sweep it into a top knot and tie it in place. I would actually recommend waiting to undo it until you've arrived at the venue. When you undo the knot, your hair is going to fall into big, soft, Victoria's Secret supermodel waves and every other woman there is going to wish she had your hair.

The Side Plait

Another look that's immediately trendy, feminine and romantic is the side plait. Indian girls are used to tying braids for school, so most of us can pull off this style ourselves without any help. Plus, it's not meant to look like you're trying to impress the teacher, so the messier the better. Most girls in our country have mid-length hair with lots of layers, which works well for this style, because the messy look comes along without too much effort. Some talented and patient women even manage to get the Heidi milkmaid braid, where the plait wraps across the top of your head like a headband. Though, I probably need some practice before I try that look out myself.

TRICK! Braiding your hair into a side plait is a little more difficult than one that goes straight down the back. The trick is to comb all your hair over to one side, and tie it with a band at the spot where the plait will begin. This way, it won't keep slipping out of your hand forcing you to start again. As you begin to braid the hair, make sure it's as tight as possible, because as you move around, it's only going to get looser. Once you've braided it down to the very end, fasten it before you take off the band at the top.

Hair Care

- I usually **WASH** my hair every alternate day though shooting can mess up this schedule. If I need straight silky hair for a sequence, then I have to wash it daily because the hot spotlights in the studio aren't going to spare me. That might dry out your hair so I wouldn't advise it for everyone. But keep your hair clean at all times!
- Eating the right **DIET** is the key to great hair. I make sure I eat plenty of avocado, dal, peanuts, fresh fruit and green vegetables to give my hair all the vitamins and minerals it needs to stay healthy and long and shiny. If you are a non-vegetarian, do include fish and chicken breast in your diet as those will also promote hair growth.
- **OILING** is great for all hair, whether natural or treated. Pompy makes a special blend of almond, coconut, olive, and castor oils for my hair. Massaging my scalp with it boosts circulation and busts the stress of a hard day. My roots get healthier, my hair looks shinier. It's so refreshing that you can see the results right after the first use! If you aren't a fan of hair oil, try hair masks. They are packed with natural oils and butters to condition your hair inside out. Kerastase's

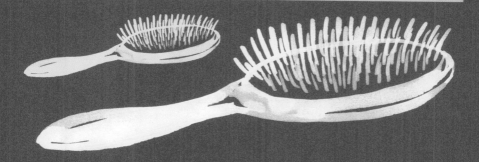

The Messy Bun

To be completely honest, when I'm on my own and there's no Pompy to bail me out, the look I resort to the most is a messy bun. This basically involves sweeping all my hair into a knot and tying it. I don't even bother using a comb, because that actually gives it texture, and I don't look like a strict librarian. This is also the best possible remedy for those 'bad hair' days when you have no time to wash or style and don't know what to do. It's simple and effective and gives you a relaxed laidback look. Throw on a pretty headband and nobody is going to be any wiser.

Masqueintense and TiGi's Treat Me Right are worth sampling.

- Split up with **SPLIT ENDS** by trimming your hair faithfully every three or four weeks. Even if you're trying to grow your hair out, you don't want it to look wild and unhealthy. So getting a few centimetres chopped off every month will help your hair look beautiful and healthy and stay in shape too.
- Bad news: you cannot escape **DANDRUFF**. Good news: you can control dandruff. All it needs is a little extra care. Use a good zinc-based shampoo like Head & Shoulders but don't wash your hair every day; that will dry out your scalp and only make things worse. Avoid irritating the scalp with excessive products so keep your hair routine simple. Dandruff thrives in high-stress lifestyles, so go for stress-busters like yoga and massages.
- The **SUN** damages your hair just as much as it harms your skin, especially if you've teased your hair with chemical treatments. Instead of letting your beloved locks get fried when you're out on a picnic or taking a bike ride with your man, don a cool fedora or a stylish scarf to protect your mane.

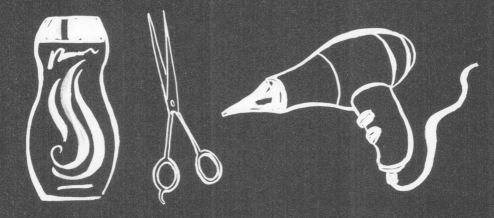

Treat According to Type!

DRY AND DAMAGED Stay away from the blow-dryer as much as possible. Try not to give in to the temptation of colouring your hair again, even if it means exposed roots. Getting a haircut will always improve the hair texture, because you're getting rid of the most damaged parts. Your hair is begging for moisture at this point, so make sure you feed it with plenty of oil massages and moisturizing shampoos.

FINE AND FLAT There are some hair conditions that are genetic, so there's very little you can do to change it completely. I have fine hair too. Although I make sure my diet and sleep routine is in place, the only thing that works is a regular layered haircut that adds bulk. And of course my favourite, the bouncy blow-dry. Volumizing shampoos work for everyday use when you don't have the patience to set up the blow-dryer. Avoid growing your hair too long, because the excess weight will make it sit absolutely flat on top.

FRIZZY Avoid rubbing your hair with a towel, because this causes static and makes the frizz even worse. Serums usually help calm the hair down a little. You will definitely need to use an intense conditioner, which you should leave on for at least a few minutes before washing it off in the shower. This will add weight to the hair, so that it doesn't turn into a desi afro.

THICK AND FULL While the rest of us are probably green with envy, there is actually such a thing as too much volume. Get a layered haircut that reduces the bulk, so that your face doesn't have to hide behind your massive mane. Your hairstylist will probably use techniques like feathering to thin it out towards the ends. Leave-in conditioners are also very helpful for taming your wild mane.

Colour Me Right!

After years of experimenting, I've now decided to stick to different shades of brown for my off-screen and on-screen looks. In *Kambakkht Ishq*, I played a supermodel where I had to be loud and glamorous, and a lighter copper tone worked best for the character. In *Kurbaan* and *Bodyguard*, my characters were simpler, so I went for darker shades of chocolate brown. For *Heroine*, we needed to up the glamour so Pompy gave me a luxurious ebony brown and added brightness with highlights. But even though I'm playing a character, the hair colour has to first and foremost suit my complexion. Keep this in mind when picking your colour:

FAIR Go for deep reds and dark blonde without it looking too fake or severe. But Indian skin has yellowish undertones to it, so make sure that even the light colours you pick have warm tones in them. **WHEATISH** You can carry off chocolate brown, walnut, even chestnut shades without any trouble. The colour you should avoid is red, because it's so warm and strong that when it frames your face, it can make the skin look grey. **DUSKY** Usually means you have very dark hair, which is a problem in itself since its natural colour is too strong to catch another colour. Introducing a lighter shade usually involves bleach, which can be very harmful to the hair's texture. Unless you're willing to take that risk, stick to highlights in browns and reds that can lighten and add depth to the hair, while using only a few strands. Stay far away from lighter brown and blonde shades; it will make you look too stark and can take attention away from the face.

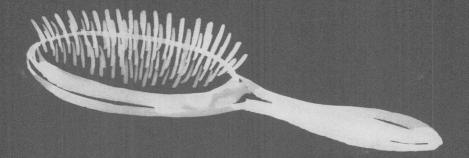

SKIN DEEP

I haven't used a face wash in six years. Shocked? Earlier, I used a Lancôme face wash in the summer because Mumbai's heat and grime can leave your skin pretty greasy. But six years ago, I had a eureka moment. Turns out, splashing my face with lukewarm water and patting it dry with a soft cloth has exactly the same effect as applying the priciest skin products. I couldn't believe it myself.

That doesn't stop me from buying beauty products like most other women. If I'm anywhere near a Body Shop store, I magically gravitate inside and splurge on tonnes of exotic smelling creams and lotions that I don't need and will never use. Of course, I feel silly about hoarding and give most away as gifts. Which makes my girlfriends most happy.

I've never really needed skincare products. I was a chubby kid with rosy cheeks and fair skin that made all the neighbourhood aunties go, 'awww, cho

TRICK!

Models and make-up artists are famous for this and I find quite useful too. The trick is simple: spray your face with rose water during the day. It's an ancient beauty treatment that's been used by women in our countries for centuries, and for good reason! It keeps the skin hydrated and since it's not a cream, it won't clog your pores. Carry a spray in your bag and spritz yourself whenever your skin is feeling dry and stretched.

chweet'. I think I made a pretty teenager too. None of those pre-exam pimples or anxiety breakouts, which drive teens crazy. I guess I was too bindaas to worry about anything. That's why my complexion has stayed even-toned throughout.

I shouldn't take all the credit though. It's one of the blessings of being a Kapoor. My grandfather Raj Kapoor began the fair-skin-light-eyes trend in Bollywood, which would drive women wild. Both Lolo and I inherited his complexion. My light green eyes are a bonus. On Mom's side, my British grandmother still has gorgeous skin at the age of 87! I'm hoping she has passed that on to me.

My contribution to preserving the genes has been to eat right, avoid alcohol and tobacco, and focus on my yoga. This lifestyle choice has had an astonishing effect on my skin and hair.

My breathing exercises and deep meditation give my body a daily blast of oxygen and a natural glow that no shimmer or blush can copy. Any workout helps your metabolism, boosts your heart and releases endorphins—your happy hormones!

The more you sweat, the cleaner your system gets as your body flushes out all the skin-dulling toxins. It's not just about losing weight or sculpting your abs—exercise enhances your complexion too.

Yoga has really reduced my undereye puffiness, a problem that has plagued me since I was young. Bags under your eyes are so frustrating, especially when you're young; no amount of cream or medicine seems to help and they make you look haggard. But with yoga, I noticed a drastic improvement. Asanas like 'downward dog'—where I bend forward, allowing blood to rush to my head—improve circulation to this area and counter puffiness. The problem will never really go away but, with a little effort, I can control it.

Skin also thrives on sunshine and fresh air. You're probably rolling your eyes, wondering what fresh air I get in Mumbai. Well, Saif and I have our little verandas, where we like to sit for chats over chai.

When on holiday, especially in the mountains, I make it a point to go for long walks to take full advantage of the clean, crisp air. It wakes me up instantly and I feel the difference in the texture of my skin. It gets softer and pinker. Even my eyes seem brighter.

Vitamin D is vital to keep your skin looking young, so spend some time in the sun. If you're a morning person, get out for a brisk walk just after sunrise. Indian skin tans well so think of it as a dose of natural bronzer. But remember to slather on a good sunscreen to keep out UV rays.

SECRETS BEHIND BEBO'S PERFECT SKIN

EAT Most people don't give enough thought to how food is going to affect their skin. I believe you are what you eat. If you're piling on greasy and oily junk food, it's going to show up on your skin. That was one of the key things I noticed after turning vegetarian. Eating **fresh fruit and vegetables** and filling my plate with plenty of leafy greens had a dramatic impact on my skin. I would wake up without that oily feeling that you get after a night of eating red meat. That's probably how I realized I didn't need a face wash anymore.

Fruits and vegetables are also packed with antioxidants, which are great for slowing down the ageing process. A simple rule I follow is 'The brighter the vegetable, the more antioxidants it has.' Tomatoes, spinach, eggplant, broccoli, bell peppers, radish and beetroot figure high on the 'good veggies' list. If you're not a veggie fan, try mixing it up: make a yummy soup or broth or try pureeing and mixing it into another dish. That way, you get all the benefits and don't have to deal with the taste.

DRINK A lot of people have faith in **green tea** to clean out the toxins from your body. I don't drink it as regularly as I should. But when I do remember to drink a cup or two a day and keep that up for over a week, I feel lighter and cleaner from the inside. Starting your day with a glass of **water** mixed with a few drops of lemon juice is another tip for those who want to lose weight and get fresh, glowing skin.

As for alcohol, drinking too much or too often can take a toll on your liver, which in turn shows up on your face. I stay away from all hard drinks, though I will allow myself a glass of **red wine** every now and then, especially on important occasions. Like if we're travelling to Gstaad and going to a terrace party at one of our friends' houses. Besides, red wine is packed with antioxidants, so technically, I'm doing my skin a favour, right? But even then, I limit myself to just two glasses. There is nothing that can kill your feel-good factor faster than waking up with a head-cracking hangover.

SLEEP And finally, all your efforts at staying young and fresh will go in vain, if you don't get **a good night's sleep**. I love my bed, and nobody can make me get out of it until I've had my proper eight hours. Or they have to deal with cranky Bebo, and trust me, she's not fun. A side effect of being tired and having under-slept is that it immediately shows up on your skin. Dark circles under the eyes can age women badly and they're mostly irreversible, no matter what creams or under-eye gels you try. Lack of sleep also makes your complexion dull and that's a risk I cannot afford to take, especially since the camera catches everything! So, if I have an all-night shoot, I make sure to sleep through the day, phone on silent and curtains drawn completely. The only one who's allowed to disturb me during this time, without getting a yelling, is Elvis, my pet beagle.

Daily Routine

Because I have normal skin with no blemishes, I don't really feel the need to use too many masques and packs on my face. Somehow, I'm convinced that the more you mess with your skin, the worse it gets. All the chemicals that go into making a beauty product might actually damage it in the long run. A simple routine of cleansing, toning and moisturizing—the classic three pillars of a good skincare regimen—is all you really need. And the fourth pillar is a good sunscreen!

CLEANSE I used to be a fan of Lancôme face washes, which cleanse thoroughly without drying out the skin. Some face washes are too strong and suck out all the natural oils. This only makes matters worse because your oil glands start working overtime to combat the dryness. You should always pat dry. But I can't help rubbing my face carelessly with a soft towel because I want to feel completely clean.

TONE Follow up your cleansing with a good toner, which reduces the size of your pores. Most toners are spirit-based, so it's very important not to spray it directly on the skin or it could cause dryness and irritation. The active ingredients in toners can irritate the skin over a period of time if used too vigorously on the delicate facial skin. Put some on to a cotton swab and gently wipe your face.

MOISTURIZE Follow this up with a good moisturizer, one that's not light and not too sticky, before you head out the door. I love Cetaphil, and still use it very regularly. My make-up artist also introduced me to this cream called Embryolisse, which is so refreshing for the skin, especially to use right before you apply make-up.

SCREEN I'm lazy because I don't tan easily, I just get pink. But when we were shooting *Golmaal 3* in Goa, they had to put sunscreen under my make-up at all times. Even the slightest damage to the skin shows up drastically on camera. And as you grow older, the skin doesn't recover as quickly as when you were young. You'll begin to notice discolouration and pigmentation around your 30s. If you wake up to protecting your skin too late, there's little you can do then to make things better then.

Finding a sunscreen that suits you might require some trial and error. But be patient and pay attention to the way it reacts with your skin. Waterproof sunscreens are good for people who sweat a lot, because at least the effect will last longer. Some compact powders now also have SPF, so you could kill two birds with one stone.

Know Your Skin

There's no such thing as a single skin care routine for everyone. In fact, if you do try and standardize your regimen based on what someone else is using, and they don't have the same skin type as you, you might be doing more damage than good.

OILY SKIN People who have oily skin think that they should avoid moisturizing their face. Wrong! If you're using a face wash, even the mildest possible one will cause some dryness. You should always back that up with a little moisturizer, but find something that's really light, rather than creamy. Face washes come with skin specifications; look for one that's meant for oily skin. It should be gel-based, so that it doesn't leave your skin feeling greasy afterward. Using a toner works well for this particular skin type. To prevent getting that greasy sheen, which I call 'frying-pan face', you could use a sheer compact powder. This will soak up the excess oil and even out your skin tone. Look for something that matches your skin tone for a flawless finish, and if it has SPF too, that's a double treat. Lakme has always made powders that really work for Indian skin, and companies like MAC have some great products too.

DRY SKIN Moisturize, moisturize, moisturize. It will help prevent wrinkles and lines, which dry skin has a tendency to develop early. It will also keep your skin feeling soft and supple. The best time to slather on the cream is right after your bath, so that you can lock in the moisture. For your face, you could spray on a little rose water after applying the moisturiser, and it will stay well-hydrated. Avoid using soap on your face and body; instead, use body washes or natural soaps which are not as harsh. And of course, it's better to avoid the loofah. If your skin is already dry and sensitive, scrubbing it constantly is not going to help. Squeeze a little bit of the body wash on to your palm and work it into a lather. It will be just as effective, trust me. You also have to be careful of the kind of fabrics you use, because harsh, coarse clothing can also irritate the skin.

Top Beauty Tips

- If I'm on my way to an event and my eyes are looking too puffy, I wrap an ice cube in cloth and gently dab my face. It helps constrict the blood vessels and reduce the puffiness temporarily. You could also put your used tea bags in the fridge and once it's cold enough, place it on your eyes for a few minutes. The caffeine is supposed to reduce swelling.
- You don't always need to go in for expensive products. Sometimes, the best remedies for skin problems can be found in your own kitchen. The pulp of a tomato is good for removing a tan, while mashed papaya makes for an excellent exfoliator. There's nothing

COMBINATION SKIN Though this is the most common type of skin, it's probably the trickiest because there are parts on your face that seem oily, while others feel dry. And strangely, as you grow older, normal skin could suddenly turn into combination skin and vice versa. It all depends on how you take care of it, so paying attention to your body is very important. The best thing to do is use a mild cleanser, like face washes that foam easily, to take off the grime and dirt. Like me, you could even try splashing water on your face if you feel like some parts are getting too oily, without using any product. Going over the particularly oily parts with a toner, while avoiding the dry portions, could bring some balance to the skin. Choose a light moisturiser that won't make the problem areas too greasy. If you have the patience, you could even try using different products on different parts of the face if necessary.

like aloe vera for calming a burn or just moisturizing dry skin. And since it's all natural, you won't have to worry about having a bad reaction.

- When buying beauty products, always go with what suits you best, rather than your friends' recommendations. Different skin types react differently to products. So what works for your friend might actually make your particular problem worse. Buy the product in a small quantity the first time, so that if you don't see any improvement, you won't feel cheated out of a lot of money.

- If you don't want to spend a lot on make-up removers, Johnson's baby oil makes a pretty good substitute. Just dab some on to a cotton ball and swipe it across your face. It'll come off like magic.

- There is some truth to the 'toothpaste dries out pimples' theory. On the few occasions that I've had to battle a last minute pop-up, just dabbing some Colgate on to the annoying zit has worked wonders. Though, if all else fails, you always have concealer.

- Don't forget to smile. You could be having a really bad hair-day, your make-up might not suit your outfit and your heels might hurt like hell. But a mega-watt smile on your face will distract everybody from noticing everything else. Say cheese!

BODY BEAUTIFUL

My most obsessive beauty ritual is something I've never really revealed to anyone outside of the four walls of my house. It's so completely boring and basic, and I'm convinced I'm the only person my age who still does this. OK, I love talcum powder. I know it makes me sound like something out of an '80s commercial. But when I step out of the shower and cover myself with lovely scented talc there is nothing more refreshing. Though this is a habit I picked up from Saif, my mom too would religiously paint Lolo and me white with a healthy spray of Ponds Dreamflower when we were kids. Then we'd get our hair neatly combed, put on fresh clothes and rush out to play. It's such a uniquely desi habit and it's stuck with me through the years. I hate feeling oily and sticky, which is almost a given considering Mumbai weather. So somehow, bathing never really feels complete without some talc right after. What's better than feeling like a freshly powdered baby?

If that's my ultimate grooming secret, I think it's safe to say I'm a pretty low maintenance girl. My make-up man Subhash teases me saying that I'm more like a boy than a girl, because I don't get too excited over chick things like facials and spa treatments. It's probably because I don't have the patience to sit in one place for too long and will probably be fidgeting with my phone or chatting within the first 10 minutes. I always say, 'I don't believe in facials,' because my skin really doesn't need it. Somehow, I feel the more junk I slather on my face, the more chances there are of ruining my skin. But everybody needs a little pampering, so if splurging on facials, manicures, pedicures or body massages at the spa does it for you, then don't hold back.

One luxury that I'll never ever say no to is a massage. Even a simple foot rub at the end of a rough day is enough to soothe and calm my tired nerves. If I've had a particularly crazy day, I just collapse on the couch, and Saif will be sweet enough to sit by me, gently pressing my feet, while I vent all my frustration. Of course, I return the favour, so it's a proper trade-off. It's also a great seduction tool. Let's just say giving your man a good back rub or neck massage could lead to much better things . . . We're also lucky that in our country we have masseurs who'll come over to the house for half the price of a fancy spa. Make friends with your neighbourhood maalish bai and pay her well. Trust me, that's one investment you won't regret.

In fact, other than getting regular massages and having my nail technician come over and fix my acrylic nails, there really isn't anything special that I do or have the time for either. When you're on sets as much as I am, you'd rather spend your precious free time catching up on sleep and meeting the people you've been ignoring for so long.

THE 4 RULES OF BASIC MAINTAINANCE

Being low maintenance doesn't mean being messy or unkempt. In fact, the simpler your routine is, the more you can get done, even when you have very little time on hand. On a daily basis, there are a few things that I'm quite particular about, which are non-negotiable if I want to feel naturally beautiful.

RULE 1:
CLEAN RIGHT, SMELL RIGHT!

If I'm indoors, I like to wash my face with plain water at least three times a day, and pat dry. It keeps the oil patches at bay, and works as an instant refresher too. Include exfoliation in your daily regimen. This gets more important as you get older. You need to scrub off all the old layers of dead cells to let the fresh skin underneath shine through. It also helps keep blackheads and pimples away, by keeping your pores clean. Use a gentle exfoliating cream once a week and your skin will thank you.

Body odour is one of my biggest pet peeves. I have my favourite perfume which the whole industry now identifies me with because it's been my signature scent for so long. I always carry a bottle in my bag to spritz on in case it's a particularly hot day. Experiment as much as you like but find your signature smell and stick to it. This makes it easier to pair your other products so the smells don't clash. There's nothing like being remembered for the fragrance that whiffs by!

RULE 2: FUZZ FREE!

There is one thing that is absolutely not acceptable on a lady: body hair! It's a curse that we have to go through the pain and torture of waxing, threading, tweezing and shaving. But ladies, this is not optional. Especially given that on Indian skin tones, even a slight growth is very noticeable. Imagine putting on a gorgeous dress and sexy heels and then having a hairy leg poke through. No way. All we want to see is smooth, shiny skin.

WAXING When it comes to areas like arms, legs and underarms, you can choose between shaving and waxing depending on your skin type. Most of us have grown up going to the salon to get our limbs waxed, which is painful, but whose benefits last longer. Besides, now they have different kinds of wax and strips which claim to be less painful. Make sure you find a really good salon with high levels of hygiene and technicians who are quick and efficient, and it won't be so bad. If your facial hair is over-powering, waxing might be an easier option than threading or tweezing!

If you're going on vacation to a sunny seaside resort, it's probably a good idea to get a bikini wax included in the whole package so that you can try on that sexy swimsuit without any worries. Many salons, especially in big cities, offer this service now. But I can't promise you it won't hurt; it's best to do your research before getting a bikini wax. Ask your friends for recommendations of clean spas that have experienced parlour assistants. You want someone who's quick and efficient, because the less time she spends down there, the less awkward and painful it will be.

SHAVING is quicker and easier but then you have to go through the whole process every few days because the hair grows back pretty quickly. Make sure you have enough time on hand when you're in the shower or you might end

Before my make-up artist Subhash began working with me, I didn't really bother with threading or tweezing my eyebrows. I'm lucky to have a pretty decent natural shape, so I didn't think I needed to go through the pain. But he taught me to remove a few extra strays with a tweezer and that really makes a world of a difference. It gives you a cleaner look, which I'm definitely not going to complain about. If you have to go to the salon, find someone who can enhance the eyebrow without destroying its natural shape.

Women have the tendency to be obsessed with looking thin and this sometimes extends to their eyebrows. But thin eyebrows only give your face an unnatural, stern look, so fight the temptation to make them super fine. Strong brows are in fashion anyway; just look at all the models on the catwalk and in fashion magazines.

up with a few ugly nicks and cuts. Just never touch a razor to your face. Leave the stubble for the men! An epilator is a bit more painful than shaving but is a quick and easy do-it-at-home option as well. Get yourself a recognized brand and epilate away!

BLEACHING is a pain-free way to get rid of unwanted facial hair on the upper lip and sides of the face. But this is a job for the professionals; if you don't mix the chemicals in the right proportions, you could land up burning your skin or developing an allergy. You also need to keep checking on the colour so that it matches your skin tone instead of turning it bright golden, which will do nothing to conceal the hair.

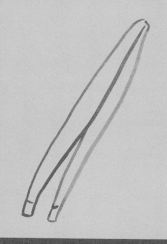

RULE 4:
DON'T FORGET THAT MANI/PEDI!

For an actress, having regular manicures and pedicures is vital. We're photographed so much that all these tiny details become very obvious when they're splashed over thousands of newspapers and websites. There's nothing worse than dry, calloused and cracked feet! You don't want your feet to make people cringe! Keep them baby soft with regular pedicures. You can even give yourself one at home. Don't ignore those feet; they need their share of TLC.

I can afford to have long nails (acrylic they maybe, but long!) because, well, I'm really not a household-chores kind of girl. But for working women, maintaining long nails becomes a real headache. I know how difficult it became for Lolo to keep up her favourite french manicure once she became a mother. You need to be Superwoman to have delicate long nails and be able to run after two little kids. Shorter, bare nails, rounded at the tips, makes the most sense if you ask me. For special occasions, when you need that touch of glamour, you can always fall back on artificial stick-ons.

If you think this is asking for a bit too much, let me confess right now I bite my nails. I've tried my best to quit, but since that hasn't happened, I've discovered the next best solution: acrylic nails! I get them done at home by a proper nail technician, and they last for about a month if I'm careful. So take it from a nail biter, raggedy fingertips are just not pretty on a woman. Especially if you talk as much with your hands as your mouth like me! If acrylic nails seem like they will stretch your budget, or if your job doesn't allow you to maintain long nails, go with super-short nails to avoid temptation. Neat and clean never goes out of style.

MUST-HAVE GROOMING KIT

You can't always run to the parlour every time you need to step out for an important occasion. Here's the must-have list every woman should stock in her bathroom for a super-quick grooming session:

- **MANICURE SET** with nail cutter, cuticle pusher, scissors and nail file.
- **BLOW-DRYER** to be your at-home hair styling pro. A good pair of
- **TWEEZERS AND SCISSORS** for a quick eyebrow-shaping session.
- A top quality ladies' **RAZOR** and skin-soothing shaving or bath gel.
- Durable **FOOT SCRUBBER** to prevent cracked heels.

FACE PAINT

I'm obsessed with kajal. OK, addicted to, and fanatic about it. Every time my make-up artist, Subhash Vaigal, comes over to prep me for a big event or photoshoot, he has to grab my hand to keep me away from my kajal stick. I plead, telling him that I feel almost naked without it, so we try and work out a compromise. I get my dark, mysterious eyes and he gets to try options other than just black kajal.

If it were up to him, I'd be allowed to do nothing but the 'natural' look everywhere. But I love experimenting, especially when we're doing photoshoots. The more experimental, the better it is for me, because I just feed off the drama. Besides, I'm pretty understated in my personal life, so this is the one place I really get to go wild. I remember shooting for *Vogue* in a gorgeous white Dior dress during my size-zero phase. The look had tons of chunky silver jewellery and my make-up was gothic and super dramatic. I looked like a sexy evil queen, and it's one of my favourite shoots because that person in the photos is so far from what I'm really like off camera. And that's the beauty of make-up—it can transform you completely!

I'm lucky that I don't have to stock up on too many products, mostly because my make-up artist does most of my cosmetics shopping. If there's a lipstick or eyeshadow that I like, I ask them to source it for me, or pick it up when I'm passing through the airport duty-free. It also helps to be brand ambassador of Lakme, because they love pampering me with goodies from their latest collections. Honestly, it doesn't matter how old you are or how much money you have, seeing a bag of gorgeous make-up products with your name on it will make any woman squeal with excitement.

Make-Up Essentials

I first tried on make-up when I went to Lolo's shoots. I'd watch the make-up artists work on her, and mimic that on my face. I loved playing with different-coloured lipsticks and eyeshadows. Those were the 1990s and every set had an outrageous range of super-bright colours. Honestly, it was a terrible time for beauty, what with everybody running around in loud lipstick, big hair, layers of pancake … Lolo and I cringe looking at those photos. How was that chic, ever? I'm glad Hindi films, and people in general, now have a minimal approach to make-up.

Back then, there were limited products in the market, and those were frighteningly expensive. I was allowed to pick up glosses whenever I travelled abroad, and loved gifting them to my girlfriends. Our favourites were cherry and strawberry flavours. I've even had the ones with glitter in them! Now, we are spoilt for choice, from pocket-friendly brands like Lakme, Revlon, Maybelline and MAC to pricier products from Guerlain, Shisheido and YSL. And then Body Shop and Forest Essentials offer organic products that promise to love your skin!

CAN'T. DO. WITHOUT. MY. KAJAL. I always have my Lakme eyeliner in my bag. Just lining the bottom eyelid makes a huge difference to your look, especially since we Indian women have expressive eyes. Kajal brings out the green of my eyes so I can't do without it. **FOR A DAY OUTING**, my look is bare minimum: just my faithful ol' liner and a strawberry-flavoured lip balm from MAC. If I feel like dolling up a bit, I'll sweep on some mascara to add definition to the eyes. I don't really need foundation or concealer and they make my skin greasy so I avoid using them daily. **FOR THE NIGHT**, smoky eyes! The look takes time to master but once you get the hang of it, it takes less than five minutes and transforms your face dramatically. It's one of the few looks that suit everyone so don't be afraid to try it. But then, keep your mouth fairly neutral.

GET THE SMOKY EYE LOOK
• Start with lining your upper and lower lashes with a dark kajal. • With your fingertip or applicator, gently smudge the liner on your upper lid, especially at the outer corner, blending upwards and outwards. • Choose a lighter eyeshadow, ideally grey, slate, charcoal or even dark brown. Sweep it across your eyelid but not outside the crease. • Again, with your fingertip or applicator, blend the kajal into the eyeshadow so they don't stand out as two separate lines of colour. • Finish off with a coat of mascara, and you're ready to hit the red carpet!

2 LIPSTICK

I usually choose a lipstick or stain as close to my natural lip colour as possible—to emphasize the pout. And it goes best with my kajal-lined eyes. My stylist is obsessed with red, which I would never try earlier except for a photoshoot. But now I'm beginning to like the way it looks. Every time we have an event, she'll give me that look and I know what's coming: 'We should try this with red lipstick…' Some people do look amazing in bright coral or shocking pink but, as much as I envy them, it's too outrageous for me. If you have thinner lips, you can carry off almost any colour so don't hold back—go wild and try edgy shades. But if you have a pout like mine, be careful. Overcolouring can be overwhelming. Stick to matte shades that don't clash with your eyes or cheeks.

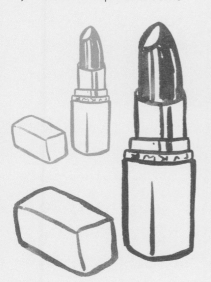

GET THOSE RED LIPS RIGHT!
• Indian skin has a yellowish undertone so look for a red with an orange base. • Chanel, Lakme and Revlon make great reds that match our skin tone well. • Prepare the base by applying a little lip balm so that your pout is soft and supple. • Swipe the colour on to your finger first and then dab it on your lips for a natural look. • If solid scarlet scares you, underplay it by blending in a pink or orange shade. • Matte it with tissue paper and finish off with a touch of nude gloss to seal in the colour.

SKIN TONE	LIP COLOUR
Fair	Bright reds, soft pinks
Wheatish	Deeper reds, shocking pink, coral
Dusky	Burgundy, chocolate brown

The one colour I really don't get is black. Why would anyone want to look like a creature from a horror show? Very dark lipsticks make you look severe so, unless you want to scare 'em off, stop at maroon.

3 BLUSH

This is the quickfix to inject colour into your face and magically create high cheekbones where there are none. I like cream-based blushes because they're easier to blend into the skin and look more natural than powder ones. Usually, a colour that's about two shades darker than your skin tone is a safe bet to get that 'natural' flush. Because I have pretty fair skin, I can find the right shades abroad. But sticking to brands that understand Indian skin tones—like Lakme, Revlon, Maybelline, L'Oreal—is a good idea for first timers.

4 CONCEALER

This is such a handy tool to hide sudden pimples, rashes or discolouration. Look for one with a yellow base—it suits Indian skin the best. Try it on your face, not the inside of your wrist, because nothing substitutes your face colour exactly. I recommend Lakme's Absolute White Intense concealer stick for fairer women. Clinique's skin-friendly concealers blend well, and Lotus Herbals uses natural ingredients. MAC's got perhaps the widest range but the best part is that the salespeople are trained make-up artists. A pimple zapper and a make-up master class? Irresistible combo!

5 BRONZER

This is a favourite trick with Bollywood divas. Mix a little with your moisturizer, spread it over your arms, shoulders, cleavage and jawline, and you'll look like you've just returned from a sunny holiday in the Maldives! In *Tashan*, Subu gave my body and face a tan base, which worked wonders because I'm naturally so fair. Want to alter your skin tone for a party? Have fun with a bronzer but learn how to blend it expertly, else you might look patchy. And too much of it could actually make you look dirty! Make Soleil Tan De Chanel bronzer your secret weapon. You can also dust Lakme Absolute Moon-Lit highlighter powder on to your cheek and collar bones, to emphasize the bone structure.

SMOKY EYES, RED LIPS AND OTHER TRICKS

Top Tips • Before you put on make-up, lightly **MOISTURIZE** your skin, except the eyes and lips. Supple skin absorbs make-up better and you won't end up with that tacky pancake effect. • Taking make-up off is as important as putting it on, so remember to **SCRUB** yourself squeaky clean the minute you get back home. Never let your pores get clogged. • **KEEP YOUR TOOLS CLEAN**. If you use brushes and swabs, wash them regularly to prevent bacterial growth. Your mascara brush, especially, can give you a nasty eye infection!

She's Got the Look, Now Find Yours!

Not everyone has the luxury to hire make-up artists whenever they need to step out to a party. Which is why I've got the basics for a few of my favourite looks so you can get your own movie-star make-up master class.

AU NATUREL It's ironic that to look 'naturel' you actually need quite a few products! **1.** Use foundation and concealer that match your skin tone to cover blemishes. Blend them really well to avoid patchy skin. Sweep on loose powder to help the make-up set. **2.** For eyes, all you need is basic mascara and light brown or grey liner inside the lids. **3.** For cheeks, use a blush a shade or two darker than your skin tone and sweep it along your cheekbone. I prefer cream blushes as the skin absorbs them better. **4.** Lips need just a tinge of colour so use coloured lip balm rather than a heavy lipstick. Finish off with clear gloss to add sparkle.

HOLLYWOOD DRAMA Flaunt your best features, go gaga on glamour, and play with bold colours! **1.** Use the same base as for your natural look, then build up the drama … **2.** For eyes, think tonnes of mascara, eyelash curler, heavy liquid liner … Try sweeping the liner up into the classic 1960s cat's eye for a coquettish shape. **3.** For lids, use shimmer eyeshadow in bronze or copper with a little highlighting powder under the eyebrow arch. **4.** Go for a deep, rich lip colour (and matching liner) for that traffic-stopping pout. **5.** Highlight cheeks with a deeper blush but only if you're already an expert. **6.** Wanna go all out diva? Dust some highlighter powder on the collarbone and cheekbones.

BRONZE GODDESS
Trippy tricks to fool everyone into thinking you've been jet-setting around the world! **1.** Use tinted moisturizer on the face and body if your skin doesn't really need a foundation. **2.** For eyes, stick to shades in the brown family like brick, tan, or amber. Line the eyes with dark brown liner instead of black but don't forget to pump up the volume on your mascara. **3.** Lips should be fairly neutral so use nothing more than a nude lipstick or lip balm, topped up with gloss. **4.** Use bronzer on cheekbones and jaw line instead of blush for an all-over glow. Blend it into your skin evenly. Match your body with your face!

STRIKE A POSE

I have a silly habit that Saif keeps making fun of. He told the world about it on an episode of Koffee With Karan. Saying the first time he saw me do it, he was totally amazed because he'd never seen anybody do it before. I'm addicted to the mirror. When I'm dressing for an event or a photoshoot, I smile and pout at myself, just to see how I'm looking. It sounds crazy, of course. And sometimes, when I look back at the stylist or the photographer, they have this expression on their face which says, 'Oh my God, she's nuts!' But I know that tomorrow, there'll be a hundred photos of me everywhere. And I'd like to make sure I look fabulous.

Even as a kid, I'd wrap my mother's dupattas around me and dance in front of the mirror. I loved taking photos, and I'd happily pose in front of any camera. All you had to do was ask. Accompanying Lolo to the sets of her movies only made my obsession worse. I would listen to the director chatting with the cinematographer and the lightmen discussing the correct lighting for the shoot. Apart from the surname, this was one of the advantages of being a star kid. If you grow up listening to intense conversations about different techniques of cinema, you'll definitely know a little more than someone who's not from a filmy background. And because I always

Getting the right photograph is hard. Some people are naturals in front of the camera. Even if they're crying bitterly with big, hot tears streaming down their faces, they still manage to make it look like they were posing for a magazine cover. It's not fair. Then there are those women who are naturally beautiful, but the photo just never comes out right. You're looking away from the camera, your eyes are shut, your mouth is open: something is just always wrong. And then there are those who will ruin a photo on purpose by making silly poses because they're not confident enough to just smile. Well, Type A can handle herself. Turn over to read the tricks you Type Bs and Cs need to become a Type A+.

wanted to be an actress, I actually paid attention.

Since I had absorbed all of this at a very young age, , I already knew my best angles, how the camera moved and how to catch the light even when I was starting out. It probably surprised most directors, because they were expecting a little diva who knew how to throw tantrums and not much else. In fact, since most of the people in the industry thought of me as a fourteen-year-old drama queen, they used to tease me saying, 'dekho superstar aa gayi' when I came to the sets. But my mom instilled a strict work ethic in both Lolo and me, and I was not going to let her down.

5 Rules to Get that Perfect Shot:

RULE 1: KNOW YOUR ANGLES

This is the most important preparation for anyone who hasn't managed to take a decent photo. Dig out all your old photos, look at everything on Facebook, and identify your best angle. It might be a profile shot, or one where your chin is titled downwards. Maybe your left side photographs better than your right. Because I have puffiness under the eyes, I need to keep my head straight and catch the light head on. That's my best angle. If I tilt my head upwards, my bone structure becomes too strong and if I look downwards, the bags under my eyes become pronounced. Women who take good photos love looking at themselves, so they already know their best angles. Once you know which side works to your advantage, practice slight variations in front of the mirror.

RULE 2: SMILE AT YOURSELF

This may sounds weird, but trust me. Your face changes completely when you smile. Look at Saif. When he's keeping a straight face, he has the ultimate brooding, manly face. But the minute he smiles, he transforms into a naughty school boy. His eyes crinkle at the sides and his dimples appear. Grin at yourself in the mirror, preferably when you're alone with the door closed or people might think you've lost it. Some people might look better with a full grin, while others prefer a half smile without exposing their teeth. Unless it's a candid shot and you were caught unawares, you can control the way you smile for the camera to get the ultimate shot.

RULE 3: FIND THE LIGHT

Lighting can also play a crucial role in the way you look in a photograph. If the light is directly above you, harsh shadows will appear on your face. The best light is usually one that hits you straight on, unless you're being shot by a professional who knows how to illuminate your face to highlight your best features. Colour matters too. White light tends to make the Indian complexion with its yellow undertones look dull and sallow. Yellow light, on the other hand, adds warmth and richness to the skin's natural hues.

RULE 4: CONFIDENCE

Confidence, as one of my favourite photographers, Prasada Naik, always says, is the key to getting a good photograph. When we shoot together, he hardly ever talks, because he says I'm his most confident subject. Think of a funny story or someone you love—it will help you loosen up, bring a real smile to your face and put a sparkle in your eyes. And there, picture perfect.

RULE 5: GOT IT, FLAUNT IT!

Don't be afraid of flaws like gaps between your teeth or small scars on your face. Remember Padma Lakshmi? She became the hottest thing ever because of the long scar on her arm, and she shows it off like a piece of expensive jewellery. Remember if you can't change it, work with it!

Pose Like a Star!

FULL LENGTH AND FABULOUS Full length shots, I find, are easier to shoot because there's more to work with. You can use your arms, legs and height to create interesting shapes for the camera, and there's less pressure than when you're shooting a tight close-up. Even the flaws you're afraid to show—tummy tyres, muffin hips, thunder thighs, can be camouflaged with the right pose. Shoulders back, tummy tucked in, and back arched. These are the three golden rules for lengthening the torso and giving the impression that you're actually thinner and taller than you are. And what woman doesn't want that? Take a quick breath, and then suck in your tummy, without puffing up your chest. That way, you won't make your bust swell up . . . unless that's the effect you're going for.

HOLD FORTH IN A CROWD If I'm standing in a group, I like to angle my body slightly to one side, while keeping my face looking straight forward. This creates curves for the camera that which

is always flattering for a woman. It also allows me to stretch my body out to create a longer shape.

COUPLES THERAPY If you're posing with your partner, the most flattering stance for both of you is to stand hand on each other's back, bodies touching on one side. It shows you are equals, and madly in love. The most elegant shape you can make with your body, when standing in this position, is to transfer all your weight on to one leg, and let the other cross over the back at the knee, so the foot is on tip toe. Look at any catalogue model and you'll know what I'm talking about.

RED CARPET PERFECTION On the red carpet, I stand with my weight slightly to one side, and one foot stretched in front of the other. It lengthens the frame and makes you look a few inches taller. Not that my 6-inch heels need any help!

WORK WITH YOUR OUTFIT Pay attention to the garment you're wearing and let your pose show off the details. Remember Angelina Jolie at the Oscars, and the sexy leg pose, which had the whole world talking. Her dress had a dangerously high front slit, and she was confident enough to work it. And wow, did she make everybody sit up and take notice. Let the camera catch the best details of your outfit. If you have a plunging back, turn your back to the camera at a slight angle, then drop one shoulder and look back coyly. It's all very 1960s Bollywood, and you'll make the men melt. Or if like me you choose gowns that show off your cute butt, a sideways pose with an arched back will ensure the camera doesn't miss capturing your favourite asset.

MAN
POWER

MY LOVE AND OTHER STORIES

Tashan bombed but it gave me my two biggest hits: Size 0 and Saif. I'd always thought Saif was one of the best-looking men ever but we weren't friends till we started working on this movie. We had a casual 'hi, bye' relationship, as he'd been Lolo's co-star earlier. We do have a ten-year age gap!

We were shooting in Ladakh's blistering summer and the posh prince of Pataudi was melting. He'd complain constantly while Akki and I tried to distract ourselves. But what instantly drew me to him was his sense of humour and love for adventure. If you ask him, he'll say I made the first move! Which is so not true because he was flirting

with me quite shamelessly but in a unique way. His first compliment to me was, 'I like the colour of your car. It isn't very girlie.' (It was gunmetal.) When a guy remembers the colour of your car, ladies, he's been keeping an eye on you!

A few days later, we went on a motorcycle ride through the countryside. I think I surprised him by asking if I could go along. The Kareena Kapoor he'd heard of wasn't much of a biker chick. He kept checking me out in the rear-view to see if I were enjoying or freaking out. It was tough to keep a straight face when my head was full of images of us plummeting down a

sharp slope! Ladakh is the perfect place to fall in love, and that ride was the moment we both realized we had more in common than we thought. Soon, we were spending all our time together, shopping for wooden boxes that Saif is obsessed with or hunting for Chinese food to satisfy my craving.

By the second schedule in Jaisalmer, everyone knew that something special was afoot. When the media found out, it made headlines. The minute people realized we were dating, their only question was: 'When's the wedding?' Before we even got to know each other well, people were willing to marry us off. Then Saifeena was born. I genuinely want to meet the person who invented this term and ask him or her—WHY? It annoyed me. I never wanted to be one of those couples without separate identities. But, with time, I learnt how to ignore it.

We are both larger-than-life personalities and it took time to adjust to each other. We had to be incredibly patient and open to the other's quirks. Saif had never dated a working actress before, especially one ten years younger to him. I'd never dated someone who had kids. Gaining their trust and becoming their friend was a novel experience for me too. Luckily, Sara, Ibrahim and I got along brilliantly. As Saif says, Sara and I connect on a chick level.

Our families supported our decision to be together, which was important because my mother is my world. She loved Saif and he made every effort to win her over. His parents were very welcoming and I instantly felt comfortable with them. I never tried too hard to impress them by being someone I'm not, and that's probably why it worked. Saif says that he knew our relationship was real when we first visited his ancestral home in Pataudi and he saw me, a diehard city girl, feeling perfectly at ease in the old palace. That's when he realized that I had understood and connected with the most important part of him.

Like any couple, we've made compromises. They've never felt like sacrifices because when you truly love someone, it just seems natural to give up certain things that annoy the other. As long as they're reasonable demands, of course! I used to chew gum but Saif absolutely hates that. We were together in a car once and I was chewing too loudly. He said, 'If you don't stop that, I'm going to jump out of the car.' I guffawed until I realized he was serious. So I don't chew gum anymore, and he buys me diamonds whenever I drop a hint. Now that's a happy compromise!

What makes us really work is that we have learnt and are learning so much from each other. Saif says I've shown him how to be enthusiastic about life, not worry about the small things that could go wrong. He's made me more patient and trusting, and taught me how to let my guard down. I got upset once because he hadn't called me for several hours that day. When I discovered that he had actually been planning a surprise birthday party for me, I felt really silly and swore never to overreact again.

6 Rules to that Perfect Relationship!

RULE 1: TRUST IS KEY

Bollywood is full of handsome men and beautiful women. Ironically, it's our job to pretend to be in love. Imagine watching your man declare his undying love for another woman. It's bizarre! But that's our job, and that's why trust is critical in our industry.

I'll admit it wasn't easy for us in the beginning, especially since we were both getting out of serious and very public relationships. Neither of us wanted to be a rebound! I'm a very loyal person and the whole world has always known that. Saif, by his own admission, had acquired the image of a Casanova. When we began shooting *Tashan*, reports of him being with a new woman almost every other day made me wary. But I soon realized how untrue the rumours were. He was warm, funny, passionate and, most important, dedicated to his partner. And yes, the 'Kareena' tattoo made me realize how serious he was.

Now, when we read about our 'affairs', we laugh it off together. I can confidently say that no matter what continent he's on or how many beautiful girls are throwing themselves at him, the only woman he's interested in is me!

RULE 2: YOU AND ME TIME

Holidays are the only times that Saif and I really get to escape the world and reconnect with each other. No pressure of unfinished scenes, box-office success, brand endorsements . . . We can do all the things that our star status doesn't let us do back home. Simple things like walking hand-in-hand or shopping together are impossible if you're famous. We'd be mobbed every second in Mumbai. But up in the Swiss Alps in Gstaad, we're only as famous as we want to be!

Most couples forget to have adventures and discover the world together once they marry and have kids. In many ways, it was an advantage having a relationship with a man who already had two beautiful children. The kids were always his top priority as a dad, but we learned how to keep the romance strong and make time for ourselves as a couple, without neglecting them or feeling guilty about being irresponsible parents.

Once in a while, surprise your partner by planning a vacation for the two of you ONLY, even if it's just a weekend trip to a hill station nearby. Trust me, it's a great way to keep the chemistry sizzling.

RULE 3: JUST YOU TIME

This is probably going to sound rather selfish but you occasionally need some alone time. Just you and whatever or whoever makes you happy—but not your partner. If you aren't happy with yourself, there is no way you can be a good partner. If you are happy, relaxed and fulfilled, you will exude a confident vibe and that is really important to hold up your side of the relationship.

No matter how much in love we are, Saif and I are very, very different people with divergent interests, and we make it a point to give each other enough space to pursue what makes the other happy. He went on a hunting trip to Namibia after wrapping up *Agent Vinod*. He asked me if I wanted to go along but I knew he really needed some alone time, so I didn't take him up on his offer. Now and then, I also like to take off on vacations with just my sister or just my girlfriends, and he completely respects that.

Being apart also gives us time to miss each other, so we're more than happy to see the other person when we're back!

RULE 4: SURPRISE EACH OTHER

When Saif and I started dating, we would buy really expensive presents for each other all the time. We would never bat an eyelid at spending lakhs of rupees buying each other dazzling diamond necklaces and expensive designer suits. Now, of course, we may not go overboard like that but once in a while, if I see a gadget that he's been meaning to buy or a watch that he really likes, I will pick it up just to surprise him. You know that look on his face when he sees it, when he sees that you know exactly what he wants, that makes the whole effort worth it.

It is vital to pamper the person you love, to show him often enough that you care, else you're in danger of taking each other for granted. That element of surprise and therefore that sense of expectation that the other person might just have a trick up the sleeve, that keeps the relationship tingling. Whether it's buying him tickets to a cricket match or cooking his favourite dish for dinner, surprise your partner every now and then, and see how it keeps you both wanting more.

RULE 5: SEDUCE EACH OTHER

… And I am not talking about lace lingerie and scented candles only. Those are always nice but, at times, the best way to get into the mood is just listening to some really great music over a glass of wine. The jazz (or soul, or blues) and the wine might just lead to some dancing. And the dancing to, well…

You know what the problem with most couples is? The problem is that after being together for a long time, they stop making an effort. Try planning a date night where you book a table at a fancy restaurant and order a bottle of champagne. It's a good thing both Saif and I like dressing up so we make it a point to deck up, especially if we're heading out for a romantic dinner. Even when I'm shopping, I like picking up dresses that I'll wear only when I'm out with him. A nice dress, a sexy pair of heels, some make-up … Might sound superficial but what it all really means is 'I want to look good for you'. That makes the evening extra special and, luckily for me, Saif is observant enough to notice.

RULE 6: CHECK YOUR EGO OUT!

Imagine your salaries making headlines, especially when you both have the same jobs! Comparisons can create major insecurities and huge fights. But we both know we're great at what we do and we're honest. When Saif shows me his films, he expects my opinion—good or bad or ugly. I've learnt how to be honest yet tactful. With *Love Aaj Kal*, I instantly knew it would work. 'It'll be a blockbuster!' I shouted. But if I know something has gone wrong, I'll say, 'I'm sure it'll be a hit,' like with *Agent Vinod*. Saif knew what I meant, but I didn't need to bash his efforts for the sake of honesty.

The key is being comfortable in your own skin. For all the glitz of the movies, at home we're just Saifu and Bebo. Yes, it's amazing to be a star, to have my statue at Madame Tussauds, to have millions of fans … But honestly, I feel most loved when I'm at home in my kaftan, minus make-up, curled up on the couch watching Poirot with Saif. That's the companionship you crave. You know you've found your Mr Right when the mundane feels like magic.

MAKING MR RIGHT, RIGHT!

Let's face it, ladies. When it comes to shopping, our men need a little help from the experts. For most men, getting dressed for an event means wearing a clean shirt over their jeans. If he's in a really good mood, like if India beat Australia in some cricket match, he might consider putting on formal shoes. But that's where it ends. Trying to get them to put on a dinner jacket or a tie is like asking them to go get a voluntary root canal. Pure torture! I honestly cannot complain anymore though. Saif is one of the most stylish men I've ever met. In fact, he's so particular about everything from shoes to suits to accessories that sometimes he makes me feel like a slob. For God's sake, the man buys antique carved boxes just to keep his cufflinks in! Now that's dedication to style.

And let's not even get started on his shoes. Saif has a separate closet for all his pairs, and he dedicatedly takes them out once a month to be polished and buffed up. His suits are all put on special hangers and hung up in the closet once they're back from the laundry. But I wouldn't have it any other way. I love that my man puts in effort to look good for me and isn't a lazy couch potato. It helps that he has incredible taste, so I don't have to worry about him buying something tacky. In fact, his opinion is the one I really value, and if something is good enough for the Nawaab of Pataudi, it's probably the best that money can buy.

Dress Him Up!

Women love shopping and men don't. Unless it's for cars, bikes and gadgets. Getting them to come along on an expedition for clothes and shoes? Not a chance. Even Saif and I have agreed that it's probably better for our mental health that we shop separately. I time myself in each shop so that I can get the most out of shopping. Sounds crazy, but when you hardly get any free time to hit the stores, these are the things you have to do. So if you have to shop for your partner, which I know you'd rather do anyway, these are the must-haves you need to invest in.

WHITE SHIRT Whether man or woman, the one look that tops my chart is a well-tailored white shirt worn with fitted blue jeans. It's the base to start building the rest of the wardrobe on, so this one must be perfect. You could blow up the bank by taking him to Ermenegildo Zegna or Hugo Boss, or you could go high-street and opt for Zara Man or Diesel. Even Indian designers make some classic men's shirts, which are surprisingly affordable. Think Lecoanet Hemant or Arjun Kapoor.

If your man isn't coming with you, carry a shirt from his wardrobe that you think suits him best, and buy one with a matching fit. Men's shirts have different cuts—slim fit, straight, apple—so even if the size is the same, the fit might vary. Getting a sample is a simple way of making sure you don't have to come back and go through the whole process all over again. And a little secret: try it on! You'd better look good in it; there's nothing sexier than a woman in her man's shirt.

FORMAL PANTS Jeans you needn't fret about. All men love their jeans so they don't need help picking out the right pair. But when buying trousers, they can go horribly wrong. They'll get grandpa-ish baggy ones or ones so tight at the crotch that it hurts to watch! Perfect trousers must stay close to the body yet not hug it like second skin. I feel flat fronts are more flattering than pleats, especially in formal trousers.

Saif's a huge fan of the fits at Armani, Dior Homme, and YSL. Among the less expensive options, Raymond has custom-fitting studios where you can handpick everything from the fabric to the style, which is a great way to make sure you get

full paisa vasool. Narendra Kumar has years of experience in menswear and many of my friends love his work. Karan too has started a menswear line with Varun Bahl and they have some very interesting clothes in their collection.

As for colour, it's safest to go with matte black. Then you can experiment with shirts and accessories. If your man has enough black trousers to set up shop, then try grey, khaki, beige, brown, navy or even a classic pinstripe. Couturiers like Paul Smith and Etro are getting quite quirky lately. Now, you get formal pants in candy colours and acid shades! It's a try-at-your-own-risk look but if your man has the chutzpah to pull it off, why not?

FORMAL WATCH Men always look hotter with a watch strapped to their wrists. It lends them an old-world charm and elegance that I simply love. Saif has a million watches—Breguet, Jaeger-LeCoultre, Rolex, Omega—and he's always looking for more collector's items. That's one of the easiest things to gift him. Invest in one expensive dress watch which, with a little care and maintenance, will last for a lifetime. It could become an heirloom to pass on to your children.

DINNER JACKET He doesn't need to go the tie-and-cuff links route if he doesn't want to. This is a simple, classy way to add a formal touch to even a plain T-shirt and jeans combo. My cousin Ranbir Kapoor and *Ek Main Aur Ekk Tu* co-star Imran Khan have really been the torchbearers of this look. They wear the funkiest graphic T-shirts on jeans, pop on a cool jacket, and suddenly, it looks good enough to pass off as formal wear. Tommy Hilfiger strikes just the right chord with this look, and his clothes are not too expensive either. For the high-end shopper, Canali has always made the most flattering clothes for men, and how can we forget the classic styles of Calvin Klein. Of course, this look comes with an age restriction. Guys over the age of 35 should just buy a nice shirt.

SHERWANI These were invented to give average men the confidence and bearing of royalty. They broaden the shoulders, skim over beer bellies and lengthen the frame to add height. Also, when every man in the room is dressed in a typical suit, your partner will stand out in the crowd. I love the sherwanis that Manish has in his brand, and Raghavendra Rathore really understands how to make princely clothing. Rohit Bal has always been great at ethnic menswear too. The only thing to be careful about here is not to overdo the bling. Indian clothes can be very extravagant to the point of sometimes looking tacky. I'd go with a plain black or beige with a self-pattern or embroidery in the same colour. The only detailing should be around the neck, cuffs and hemline. Pair it with a classic pair of mojris and watch the other women turn green with jealousy.

LEATHER SHOES You know what they say a woman judges a man by his shoes. So unless you want all those women giving your man a thumbs-down, he needs to have at least one pair of elegant leather shoes for formal occasions. There's nothing in the world like getting a pair of custom-made shoes, which is the only kind that Saif agrees to wear. But those can be quite expensive, so you could rely on a good brand instead, and buy a pair that's guaranteed to last long. Salvatore Ferragamo and Tod's are brands you can never go wrong with. I also love what Christian Louboutin is doing for men these days. Hush Puppies is one of those high-street brands that he's probably worn at some point in his life, and they're very sturdy. I also really like Metro Shoes. You need to take your partner along with you for this one, because there's no way to imitate the fit. Make sure he's wearing socks when he tries them on. That might be the difference between a pair of shoes that's too loose or too tight.

Shapes differ depending on the style of shoe. A classic Oxford shoe with a rounded toe suits all men, so these are probably your safest bet. Avoid the pointy toed ones that look like something from Birbal's wardrobe. Also, the height of the heel shouldn't be more than an inch and a half. Anything more than that and you may as well lend him your stilettos.

Groom Your Man!

Grooming for men is really very simple: keep it clean. Unlike women, they don't have to worry about waxing, threading, facials, pedicures, manicures, and all that comes with territory. At best, they'll get a shave once every three or four days. Which is really not too much to ask for. Men today though are actually becoming more concerned about their appearance, and opting for facials and mani/pedis too. Which is fabulous, but there are a few non-negotiable grooming demands that I have to put my foot down on.

TRIM THAT BEARD Kissing men with thick beards or scratchy stubble is injurious to your health. It's also disgusting to see men dining at restaurants, with little crumbs and drops of curry in their beards or moustaches by the end of the meal. But if your partner insists on keeping his facial hair because it makes him feel like a man, then you should demand that he keeps it trimmed and neat.

WASH FEET AT LEAST TWICE A DAY There's something about men and smelly feet that I've never understood. Maybe it's because they sweat more, and wear closed shoes all day. But there's nothing worse than your house or car stinking of feet. It makes my skin crawl just thinking about it. If this is a problem that affects your partner, ladies, there's no need to keep quiet just because you might hurt his feelings. You're probably not the only one who has to suffer, and other people might not be as polite. Buying him 100 per cent cotton socks—that might help. You also get foot deodorant that you can spray on directly on the feet and on the insides of his shoe to get rid of any unwanted odour.

NO EAR OR NOSE HAIR I don't even need to explain how unsexy this looks. Buy him a nose and ear hair trimmer; there's no shame in it. If you're feeling uncomfortable to ask, just imagine what he'd say if you went a month or two without visiting the parlour…

COLOGNE EXAM Smell is a very powerful attractor for women. It can also be an equally powerful turn-off. Since men naturally have more body hair than women, they really need to pay attention to keeping themselves clean and fresh. I like the idea of you gifting your man a grooming kit, where the aftershave lotion, shaving cream, shower gel and cologne all have the same smell. He'll have a signature scent, and you'll have the best-smelling man in the room.

MANE MAINTENANCE Since most men keep their hair short, they need to visit the salon more often than women. We usually go about once every two months, but he probably needs to make his a monthly visit. Even if he wants to grow his hair long, which is always a risky move, it needs to be trimmed regularly or he'll look like an ageing hippie. On the subject of hair colour, I'm a bit torn. Covering up greys with a shade that matches his natural hair colour is fine, and probably makes him feel younger and energetic. But streaks of blonde or green? Absolutely not.

GIFTS OF LOVE

When Saif and I first started dating, we used to buy each other gifts all the time. There didn't even need to be an occasion for us to splurge on something super expensive. Buy presents for me is easy: diamonds, diamonds, diamonds. Every time Saif asks me what I want for my birthday or our anniversary, all I say is, 'You don't have to buy me much. Diamonds will do.' But he's a little more complicated. One, he has very expensive taste. Nothing less than the best of the best for this royal. Two, he likes his stuff to be unique, custom-made and limited edition. This is not easy to pull off if you're trying to surprise him. But I've picked up a couple of tips along the way, which should help you find your man that perfect gift.

Things He Loves that You Can Love Too!

A BIG SCREEN TV where you can watch Desperate Housewives and he can watch Formula One. Only, don't put this in the bedroom, or you can kiss your sex life goodbye. **A STATE-OF-THE-ART SOUND SYSTEM** Men are obsessed with high definition everything, including sound. Get him one that he can blow the roof off with. He'll be so excited he might even put on your favourite music and dance you around the living room. **MEMBERSHIP TO THE CLUB WHERE HIS FRIENDS HANG OUT** Never forget the saying, 'Buddies before babes'. OK, the real saying may be a little different, but that's too X-rated to put in a book. Showing him that you want him to spend time alone with his boys will make you the coolest girlfriend or wife in the gang. And of course he'll want to show you off just to make everyone else jealous.

Five Gift Faux Pas!

Sometimes we just don't get men! Stay far away from this list. Coz he'll hate it and all you're going to get is a polite thank you: **1.** A tie. **2.** Tickets for a romantic movie followed by dinner at the new five-star restaurant. **3.** A couples' massage at the spa. **4.** A surprise dinner party with a couples-only invite. **5.** Flowers and Candy!

Get It Right for Mr Right!

• Women love jewellery, men love everything else! If he's an outdoors guy, a swiss army knife or a pair of hiking boots will make him far happier than a nice shirt. Even if he goes camping only once a year and desperately needs something to wear with his suit. Think about **HIS INTERESTS**—cricket, single malts, cars, computers—and find something to match, which also suits your budget. The thought that you cared enough to encourage his hobbies will make him so happy he'll definitely return the favour.

• Once you zero in on what you want to buy him, do some **RESEARCH**. There isn't a bigger damp squib than having him rip open the packaging of his new cell phone, only to discover it's already out of style because the latest version was launched the night before.

Men obsess over their purchases, dissecting and analysing them down to the last detail before taking the plunge. If you want to impress him, you'll have to put in the same effort.

• When in doubt, go with **TECHNOLOGY**. Here's the biggest secret you need to know about men: they never really grow up. Give an adult man the hottest gadget of the moment to play with, and he'll be just as happy as a five-year-old.

• Sometimes, a cool experience works just as well as an actual gift. There are tons of gifting companies now that allow you to plan an **EXPERIENTIAL PRESENT** whether it's taking the latest Audi for a test drive or heading out to a micro-brewery with his buddies. This kind of gift is thoughtful and original, and will definitely get you maximum returns.

PHOTO CREDITS

PAGE 129
PHOTO COURTESY Pritish Nandy Communications
MAKE-UP Ritesh Naik
HAIR Rashida

PAGE 130
PHOTO COURTESY Illuminatti Films
MOVIE *Agent Vinod*
MAKE-UP Ritesh Naik
HAIR Pompy Hans

PAGE 147
PHOTO COURTESY *Vogue* India
PHOTOGRAPHER Suresh Natrajan
MAKE-UP AND HAIR Mickey Contractor

Page 148–149
PHOTO COURTESY *Cosmopolitan* Magazine
PHOTOGRAPHER Jatin Kampani
MAKE-UP Mallika Bhatt
HAIR Pompy Hans

PAGE 150
PHOTO COURTESY *Hello!* Magazine

PAGE 167
PHOTO COURTESY *Hello!* Magazine

PAGE 168–169
PHOTO COURTESY Yash Raj Films
MOVIE *Tashan*
MAKE-UP AND HAIR Subhash Vagal

PAGE 170
PHOTO COURTESY Globus

PAGE 187
PHOTO COURTESY *Vogue* India
PHOTOGRAPHER Prasad Naik
STYLIST Anaita Shroff Adajania
HAIR Seiji Yamada
MAKE-UP Florrie White

PAGE 188
MAKE-UP AND HAIR Anil Chinappa

PAGE 189
PHOTO COURTESY Dharma Productions
MOVIE *We Are Family*
MAKE-UP Ritesh Naik
HAIR Pompy Hans

PAGE 190
PHOTO COURTESY *Vogue* India
PHOTOGRAPHER Prasad Naik
STYLIST Anaita Shroff Adajania
HAIR Seiji Yamada
MAKE-UP Florrie White

PAGE 207
PHOTO COURTESY Metro Shoes
PHOTOGRAPHER Prasad Naik
MAKE-UP Mallika Bhatt
HAIR Pompy Hans

PAGE 208
PHOTO COURTESY *Vogue* India
PHOTOGRAPHER Prasad Naik
STYLIST Anaita Shroff Adajania
HAIR Seiji Yamada
MAKE-UP Florrie White

PAGE 209
PHOTO COURTESY *Cosmopolitan* Magazine
MAKE-UP Mallika Bhatt
HAIR Pompy Hans

PAGE 210
PHOTO COURTESY *Hello!* Magazine

PAGE 227
PHOTO COURTESY Lavie Handbags
MAKE-UP Mallika Bhatt
HAIR Pompy Hans

PAGE 228–229
PHOTO COURTESY Metro Shoes
PHOTOGRAPHER Prasad Naik
MAKE-UP AND HAIR Subhash Vagal

PAGE 230
MAKE-UP AND HAIR Anil Chinappa

PAGE 247
PHOTO COURTESY Illuminatti Films
MOVIE *Agent Vinod*
MAKE-UP Ritesh Naik
HAIR Pompy Hans

PAGE 248–249
PHOTO COURTESY *Cosmopolitan* Magazine
PHOTOGRAPHER Rohan Shresta
MAKE-UP Mallika Bhatt
HAIR Pompy Hans

PAGE 250
PHOTO COURTESY *Vogue* India
PHOTOGRAPHER Prasad Naik
STYLIST Anaita Shroff Adajania
HAIR Seiji Yamada
MAKE-UP Florrie White